W9-ACH-924

Travels of the Prince

a fantasy

by John Berry

1st Books- 05/17/01

Acknowledgements

Ten sections of *Travels of the Prince* were first published in *The Beloit Poetry Journal* under the title "Ten Poems From Ananda Mahadev. Autumn, 1959

Two sections of *Travels of the Prince* were first published in *POETRY* under the titles "To the Widow's Castle" and "Winter Palace." January, 1960

One section was first published in *Accent* under the title "Koan." Autumn, 1959

One section was the first published in *Approach* under the title "The Austere Ones." Spring, 1963

One section was first published in *Manhattan Poetry Review* under the title "Zenobia of Palmyra." 1990

Permit me not

To recount familiarly

Of what unfolds,

Since it is not a vision

Compassed but a

Unity apprehended.

I have taken no vows.

My theme is princely love.

THE PROVENANCE OF DARKNESS

When a Prince mistrusts his gift,

What is there left?

A War, a Way, a Journey through

The modalities of the trance --

Reason, passion and the faculties --

To the Khan: not a fond

Presumption of palaces,

But as it were,

The referent of thrones.

KRISHNA THE PRINCE

Ascending seven levels

His own nature to rehearse,

And destiny within

The strife that motivates --

Whose sentinel was he

In the seventh phase

Where death and light concur,

If not the Khan's?

When by the light of the Dog

Our vengeful arms

Weighted the red plain

And on the Tree

Gigantic souls

With sealed eyes extended

Their blanched thighs

And were whirled by the Wind

One by one

To the westward constellations,

Frail,

Frail were we all

With this flawed Prince

And cause of his own fall,

Accompanied though alone

By Love and the Adversaries,

Worm and Sun,

Snake and Dog,

And Moon,

The Schismatics.

From guarding the tombs

The Prince returns --

Krishna so young,

So barely born.

Thunder shudders the yews;

From the bivouacs

Of the silent Foe

He hid on a dying hill.

The world opens behind him

Steadily,

A shadow stands

In a flame,

Holding a heart, burning,

Burning.

He feared,

Crossing many seas,

Many oceans,

Shores of his young youth,

And the Sun at his side

Filled with timely rage

At the Worm.

Passing those provinces

And every test but one,

In the seventh form

Received then the wound

That made him know;

And so came to this place.

Out of the cage of time,

Seven times seven,

Myself though goldfinch

Tell in each ascent:

A tale of phoenix

In the Prince's hand

As he goes up the Mountain

At Worldsend.

Love bids me sing

Thoughtfully --

The Word twines in

The dark hair of my soul,

Curbing her till

Her throat, gleaming, pales,

The eyes start in fear
Of unseemliness, the
Nostrils flare, and
The blue abbess lips
Part in the cry of
A city that is taken!

During the long
Season of one night,
While the War pauses
For the Games at Worldsend,
I will inhabit your wilderness
With your city;
Apportion the labor
And give justice;
Name all things;
Render the Khan his Prince;
Rest then in my flames.

In a dun and beggar's month
The Khan's son turned sober
In Turncoat Town,

Hooded the royal head,

Body clouded under

A dun and beggarly cloak,

Hoarding a gift of Baladev,

The raven-hilted knife,

Sought that Wierd.

Around the Capitol

Of the First Realm,

Provenance of Darkness,

By the prowling shore

He hunted; crept down

The long night of the Foe,

Through the pit Chaos,

Coals underfoot and swords.

A supple multitude will swim

In that City

And follow the Wierd

Till the Destroyer,

Passing, tears from him

His grave heart and

There is light everywhere.

Came to the hirsute river
Paler than grass and
Tempter of all heresies.
First he rounded the
Low-lying estuaries,
Till there leaned on him
Rustling reeds,
Pointing him to
The smithy of Ocean Stream,
Wind-seed couriers,
Free drifters who had
The two canons of air and sea.

Hid in light,
They left no histories,
Water and air
The way and fate of them.
Taking his word,
They sped forth by day.

Powers summoned,
Turned he then
To the heinous town,

7

The webbed, the doomed

Town, the hooded,

Searched it for Baladev.

The Foe's men spied on him

From tower and bridge,

Glinting through slits

In the stone leaves.

When the lamps of his blood

Were luminous they

Sung to him urgently

Of a rebel prince

In a black field

Digging a duke's bed.

He turned to the Manyfolk --

Disloyal to Baladev:

Till there spoke one

Learned in genealogy --

Astrologer, the blind one,

Conning the Sun through

The doctrine of air:

"I who foretold him

A great abasement, even

While he brought

Fountains of nebulae

To the birth-blinded,

Foretell you now

A falling of Realms

When the hunted turns."

"Prophesy then

A stroke of life

And the return

Of Krishna the Prince

To the one place

Where he is known!"

"Krishna the unborn

Will go up the Mountain,

Will go into the Castle,

Will draw near

Upon a broken ramp...."

"Therefore in darkness month

When all flee from me,

Weigh the adventure

Of another day:

Blindly reveal the

Jail of Baladev!"

"The Tree of Time

Grows here below.

There Baladev warned you;

There Kaliya

Of the prior race

Foretold nothing but

Recalled you to

Unsafe localities

And the bridling Worm....

This loyalty I'll repent

When death eyes me.

A devilish star will

Claw my upturned face,

Though my words fawn him

With profundities

Of considered grace.

However lean close:

There came by, speaking,

The double pride

Of Snake and Dog

Chained in and out.

North-northeast they took him."

Through shades of men

In shade of trees,

Who feared the streets

Where even the blind

Are ill content,

Prince Krishna went.

With two-wayed wile

They talked of one

To clear deeds given

And to venery, but

Withheld from the Khan's son

Their arms, their face, their fate;

Doomed themselves

To his disregard.

Down a wide street

Where the lamps were sad,

They who were there

Pointed east and west,

Averted laughter

In shifty speech.

Clothes in complicity

With guile, how fading few

Those loyal to the Khan!

From the pale midgard

Lips of couriers a

Murmuring as of dead

Leaves followed him.

Over the towers,

A dome of cloud,

Fired the color

Of burning tar.

In palanquins,

In bird- and moth-winged craft

They drove down

To soules deth

Forgetfulness of men.

Brain seared by the day,

Wrinkled of eye,

When the dream was too real

They fled away

To Dis of the Nine Gates,

The frivolous town

Of the shaking light

And the chained Sun

But the wind of the air

And the love of the earth

And the food in that coign

He called dark.

Under a blind tree on

The avaricious shore

All who had lain

Too long impious by Ocean --

The petals of a black

Flower folded inward --

Around them soon will curl

The sleek moray:

"What is the cause of

The First Realm's decay?

"Not pride but Baladev!

Dukeless we lie, a

Provocation to any power!"

"He's come to rest in rain,

A prisoner eclipsed, exile of

A forgotten tongue.

The Golden Head shall

Follow the hinge-bent Hag.

These stars shot down in flight

Light up the error of the Khan --

Kaliya the archer!"

"Krishna," the brazen boy

Struck them a solitude,

"Walks now by night

Where no man has inquired.

He takes thought ever

Among you in Turncoat Town."

A pale flame fleeting forth

Divided the divided, left

Them aswerve, unsaved.

"I was a well-treated slave,"

14

One slid to him from among the trees,

"But now your word singed me --

Look in the House of Roots,

In the fire-graven hills,

In burned ravine.

Hound by the wall, Python Kaliya

Deals a nine-door spell

On our Wierd and

Gardener Doge, Baladev."

Into the fire-graven

Hills over the City Dis --

Deathly muteness,

Desolation by a lute reviled.

Krishna came to the lodge

Of twisted roots, spied

Through a window-loop

The Wierd afloat on a dark

And withering trance.

By the fire,

Limbs of the ancient power,

Lord of the Moondoor,

Of the burning breast,

Kaliya the Pythoner!

Around him, forms of beasts

Fawning , awaited the

Embezzled blood of Baladev.

Krishna so new in strife

Leaped in among them.

Beasts snuffled him.

With the jewel-wroth blade

He cut the bonds of his Wierd.

Idiot-pale Baladev, the Duke,

Blood flowing again in him,

Turned on the Brutemaster,

But a beast howled

With notion of death,

And the trap sprung.

Swarthy forms

Bruised the boy.

The Great Wierd fled

As thought flees the substance

To return master of itself

And of substance;

Leaving the Prince

Captive in his stead.

Blood of torches

Spilled out on the hills,

Presumptuous blood

Of nightward arteries,

Blue and red, self-blinding white,

Ravening for the Wierd.

Force bloomed again in

The learned heart of that Duke.

Strenuous laughter arched from him,

Tiger over the desolation,

Sending fear into white of eye.

On the slope, ashout,

They search for comrades.

"The Dog is abroad!"

In the House of Roots,

By the glowering Worm,

Krishna smiled in the Duke's bonds.

Down to the luminous shoal

Of the Capitol ran the Wierd,

Poised gigantic on hills.

Spears and hours failed from him,

All spite and despicable death.

His fame flowered while he

Stood by a doorway

Silent in the fated town,

Resting and reckoning.

His beacon of golden hair

Summoned by lamplight

Many a wierd noctule:

Mumbling fealty from

The occult cells, they

Dived back in darkness

Till the night would go.

One brought him word:

"In a Widow's Castle

Are seven Lords,

Their fleets at anchor

Drained by moonlight

Over a milky sea,

Through the Five Atmospheres."

So he left those

Who would not move from

The Circle of Time, but

Sank in war's fountain

Downward dreaming

Still untroubled dreams

Of daughters and sons.

Baladev north from Dis

Along the sea-bight,

Shuddered with spell-filth

And the chequered town,

Came then to the violet sea.

Waves in revery,

Sun to sinister hand

Exalted and

The color of pale lightning.

Wind sprang,

Bearing a glittering sand

Back to Ocean.

Down the stairs of that foam

Stepped naked,

God of the returning gaze;

Deep-laved,

Sea-script the leg-hair;

Breasting.

A golden otter swam

Through the sea-vines.

As of lion,

Sejant;

On reef reclining,

Combers about him,

Golden Baladev,

Breast garlanded

By sea-foam,

Dividing the destinies of waves.

Northerly fair,

Weaving war

On the tide,

Word out of world-mouth.

The night-breeding Manta

With heavy wings

Warped round him,

Lured groin to wave-lust.

Rolled, lulled on hydroptic isle,

She, reef into Manta,

Full-fed orb at his throat,

Thighs tossed,

Turned them,

Disingenuous:

Seed-bloom in green current,

Alive but aside,

Fecundation of seas

Dispersed with his arrows.

Brats born in sou'wester,

Seamen armed,

Spring out of wide-wombed Ocean

And Baladev.

Thumb to gross orb,

Black blood issued.

Blocked, blinded,

She rent back from the god,

Ravening, bat-wing

Threshing the depths;

Trailed smoke-blood

From the loathed shoal.

Sea-foam

Ringed her descent.

Golden Baladev

On salt-wreathing foam,

Breasting the breakers,

Wound washed on the usurious shore.

The slim Wierd

Rising from desolate beach,

Forced northward passage

Through the Second Air.

On his back

Slow sober rain rustled,

Cloud, wind and rain

Were his wings

As he went,

Threading sea-gale,

Cirrose black,

Sky-cirque

Over sea disconsolate;

Headland athwart

The Gulf nimbus;

Bivouacs along the hills,

Alarm for the Golden Exile.

Beam of coastguard,

Rain percing,

Caught him;

Inquiry of light,

The Snake's fire,

Questings of his wings.

Lightless, loathing light,

Swerved high, soared,

Running on wind-arbor,

Wing wide-harvesting rain-seed

Above the slow wrath of

The Second Surf.

North, flower of light subdued,

Sea-floes, he came

To that place where the clouds began.

Dawn-light frozen on field,

Ice on the snows and a

Pox of armed men on the roads.

He descended by light and cloud,

Slept that night in

The Widow's Castle.

Kaliya

Below the Black Tree constellation,

Came down from the guarded heights,

From the Root House

Marched forth

Over the rocks of the world.

Behind him drawn,

His speaking power of will

Bound by the spell,

Krishna the Prince.

The Pythoner:

"What golden mouth

Has drunk of my dark blood?

What laughter of logic

Hidden from you

These arms overrun?

A raven of hollow cry

Came flying from

The lost house of Baladev.

Here, unnerved,

Piked on a thorn of fear,

You have out-tricked yourselves.

Silent -- I hear

The wild fleet fear-sound

Of killdeer over the roofs.

The Fowl with remote eyes

Courses the Promontory."

They said: "We ran

On a raining wind,

On fens of rain.

By the dry marches walked

The conquered Wierd

In magical exile,

By the River,

By the new foreign halls.

Tenuous fingers,

For the moon's suspect!

The boulevards of the white night

Held death for us

At a thousand crossways

Of the cat.

They sought us fitfully

In the avenues.

If light stay far from us

And the moon be clouded,

The adversary is simple as a deed!"

Grey seedling pearls of light

Fell glimmering on

The Nine Gates of the sea-loved town.

"Morning," he said, "has arms

Force, forms, and itself,

Whereas I am your cause.

Lead this Prince, this

Krishna my Mansoul,

Down to Dis with me,

And on a journey."

As the Snake unfolds himself

From the sleep he

Has slept with wide eyes,

So the City Dis

From the bite of darkness.

(Teleostei by the sea-wall

Too long impious lay.)

Deployed then on the plain,

After Turncoat Town,

Marched southward,

Krishna among them fettered

By the trance alone.

As one who was solitary

He went before,

Milk-pale among the larks,

Krishna the Lover,

Mansoul to the Snake.

Riverbanks each unseen

By the other, but seen, both,

By raven and the kingfisher,

By phoenix and finch,

Rainbow arching above

The second field,

Crescendo April in

The burned hills

Where the Prince walks.

From the water

Their distances were equal.

Only the narrow Snake,

Unseemly, comely, dared all

With his eyes, o hand in hand

He walked with the dreaming Prince

Through the prior States

And marked on the rock

A smile without equal.

What charm drew legions

Into his array against the

Great Wierd Baladev that day?

By a green willow hut an old man

Stretching goat-skins said:

"I had a dream last night:

Water swollen, wreckage on the rocks.

There came one sorting and singing;

Walking in the shallows

Before dawn, singing, no face

But a wrinkled river-hide."

Swerved south on the speckled plain,

That hasty army,

Zealots flocked in

From desert tribes and nations,

Nomads and breeders of horses

In a birth-marked land,

Spying from heights on the spangled cattle,

On plowmen of fields coarse

And fragrant as their bread.

Flashing of shields

Between mountains; drums of

A black-eyed people,

Autochthon, the Prior Ones:

Their days fevers,

Their brains full

Of sun and moon,

At night the stars haul them

Over the rocks,

Hunting the inborn Snake

Of whom they truly

May be born and slain.

Their huts fall into ruin

While they contrive

For their bones not to be found

By the Khan's Dog.

All but the Mountain

Wavers under the sun

As they swarm down

To Kaliya the Pythoner.

Ledges give them up,

Fastnesses, water and stone.

When the shadows of those

Who walked upright were emboldened,

Stepping from southwest

A harsh legion grounded arms

On Midgard the Marigold.

Mango and tamarind

Steeped in jungle

Where his army grew.

Kaliya alone, as one

Who needs to learn nothing,

Leading the mindless Prince,

Went down to the Minus

Of the Seven Realms,

In Earth Well, guarded

By the incestuous grief

Of Kronos' daughter

Long her brother's whore,

Euryphaessa and her brown-eyed queans.

A full circle of valley,

A funnel of rock, lined with

Seven descending rings of caves,

Carved and painted, stood on guard,

A thousand eyes, over

A prophecy of depths.

On the brim

A dark and heavy tree,

A stone seat, there

Three Women waited.

Kaliya: "I am here."

Night spread from the Snake.

With him the image of a Prince,

Gaze of one who is loth

To look away from an horizon.

They sat under the tree.

The lady said: "Rest

From the acute marches

And the Khan's blight,

Where not a root is sound,

Nor the sweet nut of the brain

Without a worm. My daughters

Will attend you with wine."

Purpled at rim,

At lip of pale marble

That wine,

From the hand of the youngest quean;

This one gazed like a white heron

Into the Well, her heart

A diving cormorant.

Kaliya:

"My tongue is black

With the night-wine I

Have drunk for the Dog's death.

Give me water from Earth Well,

Zero of the Seven Realms.

I will descend

Into the Minus World

Whence I stemmed."

Out of heavy jungle

Through night and day

Came bloodsmen, his old lieges

Riding the cataract

Till the small isthmus of the noon

Was heavy with bodies

Between the two Oceans.

The lady of the Well:
"Let their crooked feet
Approach softly, let them
Gentle themselves to these environs.
You walk on a lacy land.
Do not march here."

They stood in the steaming air,
Swore fealty: "As our own twilight
To the place appointed, we came,
For love of Kaliya, to slay
The rider of the plumed horse
And all secret pale zealots
Out of the Khan's north.
We are not prepared,
But there will be hosts.
Meanwhile these divisions."

Festival under the arbors
Near the Well.
They lashed overhead
Their tents as one
And the tarpaulin romped like a lake

In the small wind.

They painted the top of it

As a lake to hide it,

The underside painted with victories.

The scenes moved

And had life

From the wind:

Out of a black stone

Grew a vine weaving around them

Arteries of a whole Realm.

Bulls roasted in pits;

Their stones devoured

By old men.

The fish with slow blood prepared,

A white horse was slain.

In vain the Sun fought,

Vanquished, and was divided.

Night sprang with blazing eyes on him.

Moonstruck hunters running

With gleaming flanks

In the forest;

The branches they struck

Threw showers on the

Dark scalp, pearls there.

But they spy the matrons

Drinking black wine:

Wine of the ruby-dark plum

Growing in threes,

The wild plum.

Hills freed of misers

And the recalcitrant,

Loose women question the stranger.

Kaliya the Pythoner:

"Barren or briary

Are the places of meeting

And the terms of war.

Trouble your blood,

Unbutter your tents,

Disturb the melon hour --

Remember me!"

Even and slow of tread,

In the dusk, Kaliya

Came to the quiet Prince:

"Go down with me

To the place that is sought."

Where the stone opened

Underneath the vine,

And the vine under the stone,

And the stone was

The vine's heart,

He opened his dark robe.

Folded round the stony Prince,

Led him down

The descending palace,

Into night's first circle,

Into the Well.

Minus One: Cave,

And in the cave a light,

Not a light, a luminescence,

Brown glow or grey,

Not a depressant

But an agreeing, and

In the agreeing, Forms:

Forms in agreement with their pose,

Repose not assumed but

Agreed to for ever.

Soughing deliberation

Of the Sleepers,

Sprawl of great shapes

In the Cave Hypnos.

Three Queans lay among lotuses,

With milky haunches and

Their brown eyes wide.

Into their waking arms Kaliya

Fed the dreaming Prince;

Descended farther

Into Earth Well.

Through the palatial depths

Of first beginnings,

Circle below circle,

The Python passed

Ever downward, alone,

To the black knot

Of inhabited night,

To the Dark Seven;

At which level the Well

Was a river flowing

From that world,

Out to the Ocean Stream.

Entered as into the known

The spawning water;

Thereunder inter-annealed,

Clung together in the form of

A Madrepore, rising in a ridge

Midstream, along the center,

Bodies grown together,

Coitional visage indistinct:

Fixed in that perpetual flight

When the surf begins to leap

From shore to shore,

Multitude in multitude,

Unmoving lust and fall intransigeant

In the sighing stillness.

(Far above them,

Yet of them,

In the first level of night,

A waking child lay

With the brown-eyed Queans!)

Midstream here they were

So thickly pressed in one,

The faces rose up out of the water.

This hump of the Madrepore

Divided the river for

A space of twelve miles.

Those of uncertain attachment,

Or premature, fell free,

But no more often than

The root-hairs from a young head:

Whom the tide bore out

Into the Ocean Stream --

Received knowledge

Of existential time,

Till the Manta with deep wings

Engrossed them.

Mouths embryonic and dim

Paved the shallows whereon

With naked feet he waded,

To where the river was divided.

Cobbled visages underfoot,

In the current, were

As one textured countenance,

Entranced, faint

And thickly joined.

Their hair streamed back

Over their faces like

Seaweed over mossy stones.

The silent sighs of this legion

Bubbled "Amor amort, amor unborn"

Under and about his soles,

Seeming to pray him

Walk on over their faces.

Recollecting many, on these

He trod heavy or light.

To the source of tides without motion,

Ever in motion in an absent light,

41

Kaliya came in the flood of night,

Where word and deed were one,and "I am this."

He shook the waters

Taking them in his hands --

A streaming midnight cloak

Seized by a storm.

He shook legions loose

From the Madrepore,

Armed and gleaming zealots

From the places where

The flocks on the live shore

Merged with the unborn river.

Thus were they born alive,

And the voice of them

Raised in that Well,

Was of waterfalls, of tides,

Veins, and the landfalls

That hollow the caves.

Those who would not strictly wake

To the obverse dawn,

And the impure of will,

The night-weak or the slim crone,

Shook free,

Floated out to Ocean Stream.

From the gale-roar there

(There dives the dark youth,

The slim crone phosphoresced

In sea-foam, breasting it)

They came to the Sea Hall.

There the gored Manta lay

Cursing the Great Wierd Baladev

Who blinded her in fight.

Bitter lagoon where she roiled

In the mouth of that sea cave:

Blackness without peace,

White without stillness,

In a tangle of surf

Awash with the drowned man

Unkeened, over him

Shingle, spar and frond.

She felt the shaking of

The river behind her,

The drifting renegades

Brushed her wings, she

Heard the loosed legions --

Turned like a cloud of oil,

Her wings narrowing,

Flowed blind through the caverns

Of unsight, toward

Earth Well and the river paean.

O her heart lured

By hope in the Pythoner

Lord of the Moondoor,

Till in midstream

Where the Madrepore had grown,

The monster-island rolled

Before the Snake.

The chanting of the reborn hordes

Roared through all the caverns of Earth Well.

Those left above

Woke into wild agues

At the Well's issue;

Kaliya, wading further,
Restored to the Wierd-blinded Manta
Her sight for unseeing.

° °

° °

What of the dun Dog
That leapt in Gaya's ingle,
Whom the Realms catered to
Under the form of Golden Baladev?

O dog or man, the Great Wierd
Lashed them to their liking,
Through the whole north
On the glistering snow,
Till they stood arrayed:
Gaya of the cropped hair,
Tall as a Wierd, strong as a Crone
In the ice-age of her grief unmelting,
Widow or Widower,

Clashed the dead man's armor and
Cursed in his voice

The wave-lurking Manta and

Her own bloodsman

Rebel Kaliya.

How did she rule the First Realm

With courtesy and heart?

There were horizons in her gaze

Where the Kahn had lain.

Three provinces with all their shires,

Having as one head the smiling Despot,

Sent in cruel and precious ships

The most men: that was

The Second Realm,

And he the jewel-flashing dandy Lord,

Hiranyaksha of the Golden Eye.

Treacherous in fight,

A winner in love,

Small and white were his charming tusks,

Large and black his curly mustache,

And he wore only silk,

Flowing and red, and steel,

His hooves in boots with strutting toes,

Of weapons he loved best

The sabre and a starry whip.

Phoibos Iskandar, Lord and

Duke of the Third Realm,

Was a boy well made and fatal,

His army small but cleverest.

Bright-eyed in the sun they

Treated their skin with oil

From home, then snow.

Speaking of the sea and

Things of the town, they combed

Their long and sea-blond hair.

Legion of beaten bronze,

Corrupt and strict, hardened

In the mold of a pure Law;

In the field, frontal and flank attack,

The shortsword, and at sea

The beaked galleys;

In a stern manhood,

Arjuna Beak-o'-Bronze,

Duke of the Fourth Realm.

Narada of the

Unhappy Consciousness,

Lord of the Fifth Realm,

Spurred with the hairiest piots

Ever to sit horse and

Their eyes and their armor alight,

Hearts on their iron sleeves.

Faith in the Khan kindled them,

And a lost Prince.

Orlando the Alchemist,

Lord of the Sixth Realm,

With the brown maid his daughter

Sired on a slave out of

The far Golden Horde;

His army the most feared freemen

And motley wierds.

The Lord of the Seventh Realm,

His legions teeming yet apart

Like common doctors,

Held a secret so intense

That no one dared to covet it.

He was Hyperion, Gaya's son

By Kronos, so near and yet so far,

His Realm at Worldsend

Just behind the door.

Called by a captive Prince,

Formed by the Great Wierd in one --

Oh and unknown would be

The precedence of persons, but

Realm by Realm it went --

How they and their trains

Gazed at themselves as one,

As one threatening, proud power!

Deployed in careful valleys

Of ice and on the slopes

Of the white land, and

The Fleet glimmering

Under Bird Mountain

And the Widow's Castle,

In the ice-quelled coves,

They longed for the rebel

In the willow grove.

John Berry

This augured, and the bird-flights,

They marched, fields of them

And the seas, south to their War.

Depraved Dis fell at the sight of them,

Scrabbled for ancient banners.

Gaya rode without a word

Through Turncoat Town.

The main army by-passed it,

Fording the River,

Guarded their resolve.

Such was the fame of its decay.

South on the arid plain,

Came at noonday to the

Garrison in the stone fort,

Fought without parleying till the

Rocks sheltered a litter of dead.

They passed on, the whole army

After the first blood,

Down the desert hills.

Then it was they saw the

Swart nomad pacing them

On the sky-line, far and high,

Signaling with fire by night,

Their shields flashing by day.

From mountain to mountain top,

The black-eyed men,

The star-glittering,

Star-driven men, calling

The Snake that battened in Earth Well.

O then that somber race

Welled up like serpents out of

The deep earth night and day,

Following Kaliya, Kaliya

In whose will was their only joy.

The Khan's son they left

In Hypnos' Cave

To feed the Three Queans

With his dream of sin.

The Rain began with the birth of battle,

Beyond the little hills,

Grim gear of war

Churning the shore.

The streaming cloak of Kaliya,

Black within black,

Glistened with light-wound,

With blood of flare,

Seaward or inland

He raged everywhere.

Ocean by day silver

With the Wierd's craft

And the City taken,

Thunder across eastern chasm,

There formed clouds of lightning,

Inhabited night and dread.

Stricken the desert,

Drouth of cruel ships shoreward,

Many the dawnings of death there.

To the Earth Well they

Pressed them again,

The death-driven ones,

Chasmed by torchlight;

Sweating, fought flame with flare,

Dismayed once more

At the navel of their pride.

The troubled beasts wept with flat eyes

The owl disrobed.

In rain the tide turned.

Pale as a heron in the night-bog

Lay the Prince adrift in

The cavern when the Snake came down,

Creeping the night-crag.

The Queans fled crying

Thin as gulls.

Kaliya drew near

Weary and swart,

Stooped on the Prince

And drank his blood.

Over a waning fight,

Howl of dun Dog

Flying and running to Earth Well:

Scent of the blood royal

Through all the bleedings there

Pierced that Prince's Wierd,

That hounding Baladev

And anxious Duke, in all his rage.

The scared caves made mouths

At him, the Three Queans

Whispering dry as leaves,

Leaned from their special cave,

Beckoned and fayed away.

On the night-slag

He found the lifeless Prince.

Then the Wierd in a cold cunning

Slashed, and lifting the swollen Snake

Like a skin of wine,

Gave back the blood

To the Khan's son.

What was left he wrung

Into the Well -- the shrieking Queans

Dived after it and supped

On lead and gold in midair,

Sank down and down.

The husk of Kaliya he threw

Far outside on the watery hill.

Turning he heard the Prince say:

"O you have left one drop

Of blood on his lip. This

He will swallow and increase,

So you will look in vain

For the dried husk to burn,

Kaliya will be gone," and,

"He has a destiny for me," he said,

"That leads through seven dooms

To the Khan's trial," and,

"I from these depths have heard,

In Worm's domain, and in his blood

Where coldly fares my heart,

Of a drowned shore and a City drowned.

Go where the light goes,

Flee the Manta-hovered Realm!"

The Great Wierd led him out

To the sullen day,

To face the Lords

In a victory of rain.

55

The Manta soughed in the Deep

And gathered in her wings;

The waters mounted in a range

Towering skyward,

Looming for the land.

With her claws she grappled

The rocks that underlay the Realm,

Tore them grinding forth

And vastly through the hours

The land sank down.

Heavier than tombs,

Blacker than lead,

More cramped than death,

Rain clouds gathered over

The shrinking land,

Fold on fold,

Filled the world,

At once the prophecy

And the fatal stroke,

Heaping the gloom with

Miles of waiting rage --

Broke like a bell!
Doom by water fell on
The First Realm
With all its providence.

From the veiled Mountain
The seven streams rejoined,
Rushed as one River, down, a
Swirling wall and flux of energy

Carving across the plain,
Roared and ranged and
Caught up all the lines,
Conjuncts and hierarchies
Of Gaya's Realm.

Sea and sky and inland waters allied,
Engulfed the Provenance of Darkness.
Turncoat Town with all its folk,
Towers and avenues and acts,
Lay in the Gulf, on Ocean floor.

In a southern shire,

On a high hill, and the War about him

Shrinking to twelve isles,

The Prince began to build

A raft of rage against his guilt,

So that he would not fear.

The tidal Manta gored the Realm,

Ramping with bat wings

On the Widow's beach.

Armies mounting and mounting,

Crowded the rocks and trees.

Still they fought.

The sea came, and the Fleet

Of Kaliya hove inland,

Ragged and daring in defeat,

Followed afar by the foe,

And Baladev: "The Manta

Of a thousand miles winnows

The River Ocean for my life

And vengeance on all with me.

I go with the armies, Prince,

Where Kaliya leads,

Not on your barge. Your route

Lies north-northeast

Back to the Castle,

To the Khan!"

The princely barge came near

Till they perceived her

Angular forms encompassed,

Bound and pierced, resembling

Flaming flowers and stars,

But indirectly.

The barge rose with the waters.

Realm by orderly Realm,

Such was the Wierd's way,

Armies boarded the tossing ships

For life by water and air.

Python Kaliya in the

Bloom and press of fate,

Sailed out over

The Manta-hovered sea

And Ocean Stream

Due west with a turned wind

For the Second Realm and

Provenance of Force.

Under the lowering clouds,

On a doomed hill and

The black sky rivering

On their lives,

The Lords of Seven Realms

Took counsel, pledged anew

To Prince and Khan,

War on the Rebel to Worldsend.

Leaving this wreckage,

Taking aboard things dear

And things endured --

The Widow gazing down with

Stony eyes into the depths --

They sailed due west

In silence to escape

The Manta's rage.

THE PROVENANCE OF FORCE

From the Seventh Level
The blanched owl flew down
Out of the light
Across the other levels,
Wings keeping the letter M,
Cutting and coasting,
Through the Second Air,
To the First Level where
The pale tenuous one
Lay tried by the ascent.

Careful of breath,
From this earth the rising Prince
Stood at the place of the owl.
At Worldsend he
Discerned with dark eyes
The end of the first day's truce,
The games of Darkness.
After the games of Force,
What weapons, to what end?

61

At nightfall there passed

Between the two camps

A hurricane, whose point

Carved into the plain,

Writing; the Prince read:

"Ascend to the Second Level."

And he: "I can not."

The Goldfinch swung in his hand,

Pricked him: "Prince,

That is your Force! Go up!"

Krishna the Prince, in pain,

Climbed to the Second Level,

Saw thence himself

As Force raging afar

On the promontory, and

Turmoil of the Manta's shore.

Second day's vigil . . . .

Therein vision of

The primeval blow,

Earth blazing hurled

From Sun, his flight,

Her mooning after,

Urged into life

By this birth and

Semblance of her death.

"What happened then to us?"

The finch replied: Prince,

Support me now

Till I have sung

And (reckoning in song)

Robbed for you the

Dearest honey of

The chequered Realms!

(i)

The fleet of Kaliya,

Many and one,

In the unbroken night

Of the flood,

Hurled westward

Over the Manta's way.

Baladev and the Lords

Of Seven Realms pursued;

Winner and loser fled the

Drowning of the Widow's Beach.

Sailed on the bitter sea,

Waves parted before them,

Closed after,

Leaving no cities.

Equable wind over

Fleet and flagship lay,

Pulling the wooden craft

On westward like

A migration of stars.

Crossing this sea,

Sundown: flute and strings

And the voices of men.

Boys of the sunken hills,

Morose, hugged the drowned

Girls of their youth,

Died in the scuppers,

Biting their arms: far,

Far from birthplace

Where the piney ground

Wings up out of river-chains

And the matriarch

Hideth womb-lore,

Cowl of the hoarded men:

"There on the sea's edge, " they said,

"They dance an ill fate for us,

For the Great Wierd Baladev,

For Prince and Khan!"

War then from that

City on the bog.

And where the sea air had been,

Now there was Ocean.

Wind in the urgent rigging,

Star by mainmast

Quenched their wakefulness.

Watchman, withhold us

From the meal of darkness,

Watch the backs

Of the badger hours

As they go grazing on

The souls of dukes

And turn them young again.

Wallowing and huge

Your princely barge

Hove after.

Snuffling of tame beasts

In the fo'c'stle,

Stern and bow,

Dazed by darkness.

Birds on deck,

Aloft in the rigging,

Sheltered everywhere,

Trusting in spite of wounds.

In the dark light without dawn,

Ocean lay over the earth

Unbroken, to which was joined

Steadily the sky

As waterfall;

All that was left of land

Lay in our strife.

You, Prince, and She

Crouched with owl eyes

On deck; peered through

The sails of rain.

"Each drop adds to the event,"

You said, "the notoriety,

The error of the Khan."

And She (till you frowned):

"This deep rain may be tears."

.

Morning, a drowned sun

Lay on the tide;

Then rain and sky

Became of two minds.

Krishna the Prince

Felt days and nights.

At the blue path

Of the one

The persons of day

Stretched their wings,

Others brightened at stars.

By oceanic months and hourly

Your princely barge drove

Westward, canvas bursting with

Bales of wind.

Rain ceased, our grain

Sprouted to mildew. Water

Undrinkable for salt,

The creatures mutinous.

Then stars and moon

Changed for their trial,

And orders were defined.

Beyond the Ocean Stream

A brown river reigned

In a yellow land

Where the sun halts.

Second Realm and

Provenance of Force,

Which stands after

That of Darkness.

The first zone:

Runners sighted them

And Hiranyaksha rode

Down to the shore

From the walled town,

A silky Court and

A Patriarch afoot.

Drums and gold and

Ivory beggar-whips.

Swimmers guide the barge,

Silk ropes on the barnacles.

"Prince of the Seven Realms!....

Attractive face!.... Severe

With five salt months....

Let him smile handsomely,

All may be well....

Why She's a mere child,

Paler than rain

(The well and wall of it

In deep and high)!

But oh these are causal looks,

And what do we know

Of her lineage?

The Despot is stupefied....

Veil that form! Quick,

Come with us, Lady,"

Daughters and daughters-in-law

Of the Patriarch.

Hiranyaksha bows on the windy wharf,

Lord and lucky despot,

Offers the Prince

Luck and salt.

The creatures leave us,

So that we watch them,

Not the Despot nor

The kind of luck.

Hiranyaksha smiling

To the Patriarch:

"The young Prince

Teaches the Khan

At our expense."

At last to the boy:

"In our makeshift way
We outran flood and storm,
Myself with Baladev
And the roving dukes;
But our Foe and Pythoner

Won my own Provenance
And Realm! -- yours,
That is, the Khan's --
And the Force of it charmed
My own Patriarch's eldest son.

In the mid-month,
In the spring, we came
To my dawn continent,
War waged here
With Snake and turncoat
(Master of shamans for
The black-eyed tribes)
Adept at nightfall.

Our Baladev
Coasted along the shores,

Stood off the beaches

In the shallows.

We sent word to the

Youngest son and the fierier.

Wary swimmers stripped,

Larded their bodies,

Slid ashore in

The ululant night:

Found there a

Great levy of traitors

Under the leaves and

Rustling of ambush.

So the fleet moved,

Essayed the weighted beaches

At nightfall, midnight,

Morning, and the whole shore

Full of spearmen.

Turmoil of new settlers --

They boil up out of the

Unpeopled sand and the boulders.

Unscheduled tribes, they came --

Your pardon, but I am

Accustomed to the sight.

Paeans......

Our faction small

Under the fierier son,

Outflanking them; skirmishing.

Our Baladev,

Khan's Friend, our canny Duke,

Feared to partition the fleet

For trickery (Kaliya

On the full-guarded shore).

The north squadron,

Water-borne, at noonday

Sailed in under the arrows,

(Valiant but supercilious men)

Who accomplished

Death for many;

Until at nightfall there

Was held a bitter share,

Narrow that littoral.

Through the flaring oil
On the waves
The fleet moved in;
Prows breasting the flames
Like goddesses;

Baladev in the foremost,
Gleaming, level of eye.
(Of myselves and the chiefs
I will tell at table or
Over the chess game.)

We beached the ships,
Leaping ashore,
Fought in darkness
A dark people
By torchlight
(Watch teeth and eyes!)
Woodwise and tropical;

Till by morning
Our law was piked again
In that district ....

Sent for the leaders.

Who slept that day?

The Fleet hoisted anchor,

Stood offshore, and

The monsoon migration turning late,

Turning at equinox,

A love-wind in the little waves.

Vigilant for the command

Of Baladev,

Line of assault held,

Selvage of battle, yet

A mere zone of

The Khan's Realm and your War."

They based the Court

In the Patriarch's palace,

"Since justice is what you ask,"

Krishna the Prince.

"In return for this, our

Creatures and our present self,

Give me your oath,

The Second Element,

The key to all your Force --

Or do you think me too young?!

"Justice and evenness,"

Said Hiranyaksha,

Are surely the norm;

Yet in this province

Two sons of my Patriarch

Seem born to contend,

Although their mothers were

The best of friends.

One would unite the

Districts of the north

With those of the south;

The other, those of the west

With these of the east.

Now Kaliya has one,

Baladev the fierier,

And the fight is here.

To moderate it is my choice."

"These sons, " the Prince said,

"Are they evenly matched

As to intelligence,

Luck and force?"

"They are."

"Then let them, for the

Time being, spar.

My business is

With Kaliya and you.

Concerning the Second Secret

And this War: What

Do you intend?"

"O, Prince,

That is difficult...."

"Speak, Hiranyaksha

Of the Golden Eye!"

".... am committed

To invisible peers

Upon whom all my favors

Are contingent;

Involved, you may say,

John Berry

With treachery, yet loyal.

Briefly, let us,

You and I alone,

Seal ourselves nightly

In the gaming room,

Doorless and windowless,

Lit by a candle,

Where we shall play

A game of chess.

For you must fight me;

But let us fight as friends.

If craft and destiny

Are with you, Prince,

Then yours shall be

The Second Secret

And all my Force."

"And if you win,

Lord of the Second Realm,

If you win this game?"

"Oh, then you shall lose,

And not know beforehand

What it is that you shall lose.

Consider if you dare."
"I dare," the Prince said,
"But let it be
Two games out of three."

Flame of candle
Invisible in a dark room,
And a game of chess,
Night after night, alone.

Of the campaign southward,
What news could there be,
But the line at standstill?
"How shall the untrained be trained,
So many festivals!"

Skirmishing....
Silence of battle;
Of fighters, acedia,
Weariness at core,
That cometh at noonday
Or a little thereafter.

Hiranyaksha of the Golden Eye:

"As we begin by imposing

A time upon a time, so

The game will be imposed

On our discrepancy.

I know my wile, and I

Advise you to be on your guard."

"I miss nothing.

You will know when I catch you."

"O Prince,

Though I preside here

Like a mountain,

I am not solid.

If you so much as shift your gaze

To the flame a little,

My form will flicker and

Metamorphose into that moth

Whom you see trying so

Unsubstantially to possess

The one source of our light.

Or, if you close your eyes,

Am an uncobbled play of atoms

Romancing at their lasts and firsts.

I fly pell-mell through time,

And summer as steadily

In the otherwhere

As a voyage of birds.

Yet you condescend

To play as though you thought

I were one star.

Your move, Sir."

"I know.

(Now I am alive.

In ease and openness

I take my now.

To ascend, to condescend,

Descend to be myself,

I'll winter in the everywhere.

I will not move.

My obligations -- brain,

Heart and the bodymaster --

I leave outside,

Gifts profane,

Profound and chiefly,

My moved unmover's.

Moving like waiting wings

They stir this stillness,

Urgent to bear it

Nowhere and everywhere.

They have but elsewhere.)

I have moved."

"Oh, Prince and dear

Beginner of my thoughts,

With your beginner's luck

You win! -- the first game."

How lucid the Prince

In company of the Patriarch-

And-Greybeard Boy!

They ride on horses

Shaggy and humorous.

From hills they survey valleys,

From valleys, hills.

Prince:

"Let a wall divide

The districts, zone from zone:

Earth-works, solid,

With a brick facing;

Wide enough at the

Top for cavalry;

Battlements well spaced.

Divide the two brothers,

And Kaliya from Baladev,

Till I win at chess."

Districts divided in

A double curve.

To the right the Sun Dog

And ourselves,

To the left the Worm;

Light and dark,

Man and woman and

The eight seasons,

Lipotes and mortar in the hod,

Pole balanced on shoulder,

Slanting neither before

Nor after, bent, however.

"Thus the upright man is

An arrow," the Patriarch,

"His life is a bow."

Planting of lentils,

Well-digging, harvesting.

Deciduous fruit

Thrives on old wargrounds;

Lotos will grow nearby,

And the rules of action,

Music and the dance.

"Thus I may win the game."

"Observe on the hills

The hebetude of moist man.

At the gates of time,

At the silver crossroads

Of the Snail, he

Runs his diverse moistures

In dry furrows, Prince,

To earthen lake.

Sky contains the demarcation

Of his provinces.

How many true men?

84

Let them not hope to hide

As laborers in the paddies;

Or, levy their grain....."

"What immeasurable hour, my guide,

Holds us from the breaking

Of our dismay?"

"Patience, that makes a Prince

Acceptable ever."

"Marvel with me

At your venturing Prince!"

The first rain from the sky declines;

All the clustered blenched nuns

Of the blackness make

Declaration of dependence;

Waterhoard in sedition

Among the branches.

"When the wind has grazed

On our hair,

Thoughts devour the limbs

In the hour of the second rain."

"Hiranyaksha the gamester waits,

All skill and secrecy.

And if I lose?

Yet what can I lose?

Though a novice, I

Won the first game, unless

In a trance of shame

Over the eight thousand pawns,

He let me win...."

Hero advancing

Into age before us,

Filling with trepidation

The piracy and plague of night

Wherein the soul is pocked,

Look back upon our faces,

For our youth troubles us,

We are not old enough for life;

But our twin fiend

And risky foe

Flares ahead with his own will,

And we beget, beget....

Ah, very old one,

What period of great ease

And of appropriateness

Do you foresee --

Before you, I mean,

On the precipitous journey?

What provinces? What

Service of the lute maintained?

In the drunkenness

That is our life,

Instruct our taste.

And as to the light....

"Master, let your eldest son

Come over to our side --

All may be well,

Though Hiranyaksha win."

Patriarches:

"This son you speak of

Is haunted by a sense

Of manyness

Since War and the Pythoner,

Creatures and the gift of breeding

Disembarked in the yellow land.

Although his calligraphy

Is not without fault

In the eyes of critics,

He sends me word....

There were, it seems,

Obstacles in finding

A suitable brush

For the execution of

Dutiful words."

"My teacher,

Am I not ready for a word

With my own father?

Have I not settled the rules

Have I not mastered the art

Of proper conduct?

I excel in fighting,

Navigation, carpentry

And animal husbandry....

Now, how can I return

To the Castle,

When, and by what routes

On the Ocean Stream?"

"When a Prince accomplishes

A great work, it does not mean

That the prohibitive

Is not demanded

Of him also.

The Empire's quasi-round,

And the Realms concentric,

Quasi-end in their

Quasi-beginning....

So that, to revert

To the moving point

Which in our imagining

Is still ----?

Behind you grind the

Everlasting tides and

The prevailing winds

Are contrary.

Forward with the War.

The way back to

The castle is away."

The clouds divide,

Metamorphose,

Banks of eyes

Diaphanous,

They mark well

The unreturnable way.

Silence of

The uninhabited world

When the ear

Is no longer virginal!

Sun embedded in

The naked Now,

Navel of our system, is

Inconceivably ignorant.

Hail, pellets of sunlight

In the painted air!

(It is well to know where

The navel is located.)

ooooooooooooooooooooooo

A prim palace
When the snow clasped her.
The Prince woke
To a white world,
Arose to the noise,
The grim gear of War,
The glittering chiefs,
Pomp of the generals.

Yet, "What if I greet them
Clear from an hour
Of absence?" and withdrew.

Above was She,
Her hair veiled
In pallors of the white sun,
Foam-white robe,
Seaflower burning, burning
At her throat,
Kingfishers
Circling her.
"O my lady, why tears?"

John Berry

A mere child.

Let her woman it

In the courtyard

With the daughters-in-law,

Weaving....

Myosote paving the inner court,

Palustris,

And the air,

Whether brown or bright,

Warmed; gold chain

To acacia trunk,

Tenuous, panther

(Teetering, black and

The regard pale gold,

Black luminosity,

Crystal cornea,

Thick but compressed

By the neuter passion,

Luminous under

Acquainted seas

Not wholly discovered)

Walked to the left,

Winding,

To right unwinding,

Fro, fro and to,

And the chain coiled,

Unmassed,

Coiled on the tree,

The dark gold choiring,

Choiring.

When he wound to the right,

Collection of arms

Menaced the provinces;

Unwound, new penances passed,

But light, light;

To left,

Rapid and regal music, levies....

Amethyst flower

In hand of lunar bush,

Biding jester

From beyond the wall;

Fungus, nelumbo, root

Of acanthus biding;

John Berry

Myristica, and

The vine-veined air

Enlightened by a flute;

Cockateel-flash

Over fern,

Ash of rose-pearl;

Aralia, dulcamara,

And two white monkeys

All suggestion,

In the guarded wood.

Beyond, beyond,

All snow and fields of snow.

And the blue lake

Feathered down

On the floes,

Sea-floes

Under Bird Mountain,

Under the winter palace,

Far, far,

Down the white cliff.

Swift ship in sea-mist

Anchored aloof,

Death-slim,

Sea-cyst,

Nodus of moon-ray

Floating, floating,

Keen shimmer

On milky water,

Bringer of envoys

From the provinces....

The Prince

Drew over his back

A tunic of white fleece,

Flung half forward

Over the left shoulder,

The other half

Across to the right;

Went down to

A council of Dukes.

How many eons

At the Second Game,

Royalty and the Gamester!

"The wisdom of this move...."

"A consolation prize,

A long, unwritten book,

And burnable -- Wisdom!"

"What will you ask of me

If you win?

What will you do?"

"Dear Prince,

Nothing can happen,

Nothing occurs

But the pure play."

"Why do you fight me, Hiranyaksha?"

"The answer is lost

In the question which

So vainly supplicates it.

Yet there's a fulfillment

In the Prince which is

Infinitely prior

To his desire."

"Are you perhaps

Disaffected?

At times it would seem almost

As if perfect honesty

Were not available.

I would divest myself

Of acquainted fact

And become alone...."

"Or even speak to the Khan?

To speak is to affirm

Alienation, not the

Silent harmony of kings

By which I rule this Realm."

"Hiranyaksha, are you

Essentially loyal?"

"I am, and with this move

I win the game!"

"But how?"

"So it stands,

One and one.

Tomorrow night, then,

The third game,

And it's winner take all

And loser none."

Prince and Patriarch:

The owl omens out

Of the willows,

In a grey flare

Butts the air

Back to the hollows.

"Thus came I

To foreknowledge

Of yesterday."

Your mountain pony

Will scamper here

On the Wall.

For your cavalry,

Couriers, generals....

"The drip of rain

This morning is like

The crackling of fire

In the hearth tonight,"
Prince, "and the waiting...."

Patriarch:
"The eminent friend
Is there already and
Back to back you stand
Waiting for each other
To arrive in time.

Signs everywhere affirm
The fact in the principal
Unspoken languages.
To wait is not to wait.

The Khan is also that
Inherited trait,
That agent which
Impels the Prince
To return to him.
Though you have left him,
He has not left you."

"What shall I do, then?"

"There is your theme:

Do nothing."

"Retract what I have said or done?

Refrain from apology?"

"Refrain from seeking."

"I'm not seeking him!

You have misunderstood me after all."

"Stand still, then,

He will come here."

"Oh, Patriarch, that

Would complete the blow!"

Baladev:

"Your wall and your skirmishing

Will front him off

Till the turn of the wind,

Then I must fight him.

Your battening Worm

Works on our fate.

Beware of trickery, Prince,

This side of the wall."

"How shall I mediate them?

Secret, War and the Game

Weigh on me --

Honor and She and

The sure lust of things

Divide me, Sir.

My memory is not infallible."

Patriarch:

"Here the true Prince

Is absent-minded; cannot

Remember his well-doings

Or ill-doings;

Forgets to be elated

Or chagrined at the said forgetting;

Forgets that he is;

Takes all that is given him

And lets it go;

Has no roof, no

Floor, no walls.

Infinity and the people

Find him irresistible.

Such is royalty."

"How can one be

Perennially refreshed

From a bowl that has

Not one thing inside?"

"It is simple.

When one's bowl is full,

One starves."

"Or should a Prince beg?"

" From a Khan, of course --

Properly not an asking

But a granting

Of the same royalty,

Oneself."

"The Khan's favors

Are not always what

One would expect."

"To the true Prince

Everything is unexpected.

He does not cheat

(As a Despot may)

By forecast or memory,

But like the Khan

Deals with events

By being himself alone."

"Oh the eternal tyro!

Thus I learn nothing!"

"This can be said

Only of royalty."

"Well. A virgin

to each game,

And true, my trouble is

The freshness of things.

Nothing repeats,

I learn nothing from men."

"For the Despot

Loyalty is no lark.

In emptying himself

Of himself,

He must be

Absurdly incautious.

If he makes the slightest reservation,

Nothing happens.

If he so much as plucks

At a thread on the sleeve of

His departing will,

The whole will remains.

If he takes hold

Of one blade of grass,

The world stops

In its tracks."

"This adversary

Is too much for me!"

"Give up, Prince, and win!

But I must warn you:

Watch the board tonight,

Lest Hiranyaksha

Use his sleight-of-hand."

Hiranyaksha said:

"How slight is our flame,

Yet it lights up

Eight thousand pawns and two."

"I can see it."

"The lusty candle,

Slim and stark,

Dominates us in the dark

Like our own secret thunderbolt

And counterpart.

But look it in the eye -- straightly."

Midnight.

The Prince looked and yawned --

Saw in a flicker of flame

His very king checkmated

By a move so stealthy and shadowy,

That Hiranyaksha's hand

Seemed not to stir.

"Fraud!" the Prince cried.

"A sleight-of-hand!" And he

And the Despot leaping up livid

Faced each other over

The tumbled board.

Sparkled the Golden Eye:

"Oh weigh your words.

Everything has its position,

But nothing is still."

"Movement is the

Decision of locale.

How then shall we

Settle our account?"

"The wise man has

Settled his accounts, Sir,

By calling the whole thing off.

He refuses to prosecute, he

Refuses to defend.

At any time,

Having settled his accounts,

He is ready to leave or to die.

It is all equal.

The main thing was

To settle the account.

So with my victory."

"How is the world so wrong

And yet so right?

These lies so true,

This folly wise,

These wickednesses good?

I am trapped but not tricked.

There is something about you

That is not practical.

You are disqualified, Sir."

"Whence this effluvium of sky,

This flux of earth,

This Prince! --

An independent sport

Without precedent, ah,

But with antecedent!

It is clear, you

Do not understand me.

I do not underwrite the treaties

Of my intelligence,

My sex or my ambition.

Do you take me for a half-wit?

A lecher? A tyrant?

Whichever I underwrite,

That is my trove and secret keep!

No, Prince,

I who am I do not address you,

Rather am addressed --

As the address given.

Am now this forwarding address.

Adieu."

The flame squeaked out

In a mouth of red silk.

Clang of door-bolt. . . .

"A bloody mole trap!"

Unheard in the rollings of

Eight thousand chessmen

In the pitch-black,

Butting his head:

Three days in solitary and

No victuals, for a Prince!

(Half a bottle of wine. . . .)

"What good is a Princess

With no intuition?

A Patriarch with no sense of time?

Or a disorderly Baladev

That won't win? Why,

The Dog is worse than the Worm!"

Carefully old,

The bronze-winged jaçana

Walks on lotus pads,

And the Priest walks,

Prepares with fingering feet,

Kneading and kneading,

The soft body of earth.

The mountains lay themselves

Bare to celebration,

Wind-ghosts reenact their lives

For gnarled biographers;

As many lives as ghosts

In the prowling woods,

For every ghost a birth.

Out of the jungle

From the green southeast,

Along the river,

Toward the Capitol,

A black line, a

Thing winding, reptilian. . . .

Sun-colored Baladev

Looked over the sloping land.

"Whatever crawls," he said,

That is the force of him,

Kaliya, Python and Pythoner.

Below us,

At the mouth of

This deep inconstant gorge,

In three hours' time,

He will pass, his eyes

On the unguarded Capitol.

From the woods there

On his flank

We will dismantle him

Before morning."

Treaty made with the

Fair fierce horsemen of the hills.

Descent sharp and perilous,

Through forests,

Warm waters,

Down to the humid plain.

They came then,

Wierd and Patriarch,

But not She, the Consort.

"What centuries have I been left

Rotting and pondering!"

"Your pardon -- we were fighting,

Prince," Baladev,

"Now it is done;

Hence this silence you hear.

The Rebel has outflanked us,

Gone with his Force

To the Second Province where

The Priest rules with

A feathery hand.

Ambiguous war waits us there,

For Hiranyaksha

Of the Golden Eye,

By fraud and force,

John Berry

Stole your queen!"

Then the furious Prince:
"In that hot land
I will encounter them
With a law so strict,
They will beg fire ----"

"They are born of umbrage,
On that plain," the Wierd said,
"Loyal to age
That antedates the Schism,
For oh the hoar-hearted Worm
Is my original at
The roots of Force."

"Name our best course!"
"Time, the grand felon.
For his bloodsake
Kaliya plies an
Intricate sweltering wood,
South-southwest,
Three days ahead of us,
With nine days' edge.

But I at another dawn,

In another form,

Hugging the musk-ox,

Traversed these routes.

I know a U-shaped pass

And short-cut in that

Star-tingling mountain wall."

"Guide me, my Wierd

And Gardener Doge, while

I keep watch for

The gold car of Love!"

But they came on horseback.

. . . .

Patriarches:

"When the master is painting

His own image,

The silk-screen must remain

Perfectly still,

Or there is distortion."

"Master, it is a season

113

Of strong winds; then how

Shall an orphaned Prince not be

As active as possible?

Reason keeps me

From getting any worse

Or any better,

Even at my departure.

To be a Khan's son

And at odds with him

Is to be farther away

Than one who never saw

The inside of a castle!"

"The cause of a Prince when young

May bring on a humour

Of constitutional drfting

To a vortex of guilt

Wherein he perishes;

But if the cause be

Guided and comprised

By his mere princeliness,

He may wander as he please,

Or concentrate, there is no danger."

"War is my cause."

"The most fatal!"

"How shall a fatherless mind

Reared in variety

Fix itself on its

Unchanging referent,

Or come to rest in

The unmoving matrix

Of its motion?

How shall a river stop?"

"It is harder for a Prince

To empty himself of

Virtues than of vices.

However, in the Second Province

There is a drouth. . . ."

"How shall I thus be single,

When I must

By my divided nature,

Be in motion?

How can my mind be one?

I am not yet the Khan.

Am rather image of

A Khan's caprice --

An abandoned work!"

"Is it not possible

To have been so familiar

With the Khan,

Day after day,

Night after night,

That one is in danger

Of underrating him?"

"Oneself taken for granted --

Or despised!"

"Prince, adieu.

The way and the journey

Are not the same.

To journey is to lose the way."

"It has left me."

"Then how can you find it

Till you have journeyed?

The way winds through,

Around and among,

Between, above and beyond

These forts, these fastnesses, these walls,

To where the castle is. . . .

No, there is nothing

To know here,

Nothing for a Prince.

Pass on!

Behind you is the trip

You may not take again

(For roads are moved

When you have passed)

To kiss the Stranger

You would not accost.

You have no time to know

Or not to know these things.

Pass on!

Beyond the far district

Are the mountains of ice,

John Berry

Shires of the clouded leopard,

The musk deer

And the moose deer. . . .

Perilous descent. . . .

(Yet they came, and

The scrolls undatable.)

There is a monster

Of wisdom in the ice --

But you are too young

And in haste.

Follow his river to

A luminous plain

Split between war and sun,

Water and thought.

There you will find one

To instruct you

In the second stage.

I have heard his feet go

Feeling the earth,

And scrolls portray this priest

Agreeably

Walking on lotus pads

Over the joined waters,

Like the bronze-winged jaçana."

. . . .by night westward

Through the bleak passes.

Snow land there,

Bitter and bright air,

Thinning and thinning

("Crazy! 'S'out of 's head ----

Should of gone south --- south!")

Towering domes of ice

And steeples of ice in a

Tangle of sky-storms. ("Heart's ---")

(ii)

Lumpy aether tumbled about us,

Formings of greynesses,

Earth but assumed below;

Unseen the bluebeard crests

That hung about,

And bones of hackled eons

In the ice.

Through the stiff air,

Over the buckled ground,

Up icily came we then

To Nalanda.

While we sought breath

Among these warring shapes,

Our souls visible

At every breath,

The Golden Eye

Scorned over us,

Moved down --

"Hiranyaksha,

Enclosing in his sheen

The Lady,

And where we march for months,

We Veterans up here

In a frosty train,

He in bodiless flight

Is there at will,

Delicious and low

In the Second Province."

"Oh, may her virtue keep her,"
Krishna the Prince.
We came down to
The high forested hills.

Efflorescence of jungle,
Priest's terrain,
Bird that floats
In the foreign capital
And the tiger under the leaf.

Erection of whitenesses
Oppressed by the leaf,
Spires in the forest
And the tiger under the leaf.

Here were no exiles.
Outcast, but from
The leaf no exile
But of brief duration.

Thus far we came, relics.

The others we honored.

And there are rumors

That the Khan

Is dissatisfied

With all of us.

ooooooooooooooooooo

Moon hies up a well of light,

Farward, farward, whence

This shimmering rain of moon.

A smiling man by

An ambiguous well

Reveals the self

At the level of vertu.

Neither eating nor drinking,

Sleeping nor waking;

Chaste among our mysteries

And doubtful rites;

Partial to the impartial,

Turning the Wheel

In the shadow of a tree --

The Priest. But,

"How can I take sides
In a seeming broil," he said,
"Each a variety
Of phantom, unreal,
And ourselves also?"

"Let this be real,"
The Prince said: "My command.
Give me my Princess
Out of your seeming land."

As She stepped forth
Real into his rage,
"Where is your sir," he said,
"The cheating sport?"

"Prince, did you wager me?"
"I did not." "Then
He is not mine.
When our Wierd roared down
On him and that Other -- there --

Out of that gulley of tongues,

123

This Priest's gentlemen

Eased me of Hiranyaksha,

So led me here,

Though without witnesses. . . ."

"Lady," the Prince said,

"If you are faithful,

Fire be your witness."

A burning wood then, and

"Let her come and go through it,"

He said, "With all her looks

And charities."

How like a dawn world

Was that fiery wood,

Trees a transparent roar

Or rosy gold and black of red

Yellows hierarchical,

To widow-white,

From which dread purity

Fowles fled and beasts,

Though it was noon.

Then the Priest looked

Out of his windowed now,

Lifted three fingers

Of the right hand,

And everything was

A bright listening ---

"So transient is She,

And her tears so true,

That I will help her

Sensuous counterpart.

Thus I partake in the seeming,

And let it be said

That certain things move me

As I do them."

The dying trees

And living flames

Embraced then and,

Languishing together,

Fell away from the

Path of that Lady.

A young brook

Ran before her

On the hissing ground,

Cooling her way,

And a wind in love

Brought flagons of air to her

From the snows.

So She passed safely

Through the impassioned wood

And turned to pass again, but,

"No!" the Prince cried.

"I have seen the fraud, and

Have no mind to see it again.

Suppose you were scorched!"

That night she soothed the wind;

The brook she kissed;

Pardoned the flames their rage;

For the trees

There were tears.

°°°°°°°°°°°°°°°°°°°°°°°°°

" . . . . the army unsheltered

Fighting there in drouth,

Secure them against the rain

Of these gold arrows athirst --

This is no season for spite,

Let them come in."

Warily at the far gate,

A rider of Kaliya.

To the temple is sent

A barbarous gift -- noctule --

From Pythoner to Priest!

Gold and rainless cloud mounting . . . .

"Interregnum

A time of uncertainty. . . ."

The Priest and Baladev

Stood in a hall guarded

By airy sculptures of

The Kahn as all our loves.

"What of the gifts,

The correspondences,

Priest-Governor? What of your oath

To our same Khan?"

Yellowhaired one

To the camp, thirsty,

Torn at the hems,

Bearing a sword's debacle:

"Had the tree-leaves

The shape of foreign eyes;

Were time place and

Suicide by fractions ---

Were we not dry ---

But the morning leapt

Up from those hills,

Stormed us with a

Host of red spears,

By-passed our squadron

(We heard the words of

Thunderous fanatics

On plumed horses),

Suddenly were gone.

O voices beautiful

As a purple drum!"

The dry woods were accused

That slew the solitary agonist --

Kaliya the Dissident,
Replenisher of tears,
Master of tides,
Enricher of the land,
Brown river that coils
In deep valleys.

A little past noon
By the heat, a smoky air
Lay over the armies like a sea.
Their deeds flashed
From them like fish,
Wavered into the drouth of time,
Silver with pain.

Night deepened,
War-noise slacked,
Ceased and the fight ceased
Upon an anvil quiet.

Morning come,
Kaliya's horde was gone,

Quail tracks led to the hills.

Victorious Baladev

Stood on the plain,

Doubting the murky air.

A movement of the clouds

Betrayed the Serpent's coils.

Kaliya vast and gray,

Encircled Rain Mountain,

Imprisoning the waters,

The source of waters,

The seeds of water.

"Kaliya!" we prayed,

"Python of iron in scale and coil!"

Below him, garrisoned

In stone forts,

Hiranyaksha

Brandished all his force

At the approaches to

The Water-Master.

Rivers dried up,

Every stream and brook,

Pond and well, and
No rain fell.

Under an iron sky,
The grass and we
Withered and died,
Crops and our beasts
Unborn again.

Always there above,
Old Holdfast
Knotted himself
Gripping the water-roots,
Remorseless.

We cried out,
Abasing ourselves:
"Parcher of the corn,
We know your power,
Relent now!" He would not.

The gold cicada
Burnishes the noon.
In moonless night,

131

At the white of noon,

On the grim gear of war,

Chiefs and Veterans

Sharpen their fathers' wits

To cut those coils.

Under the panoplies

The exalted slain

Refuse dust

Without water.

Still the nights are

Carbon to the days;

Sleep without substance,

Waking without shade.

Daily at dawn and

The cow-dust hour

Baladev and the Veterans

Crawled up Rain Mountain,

Battered the stone forts.

Hiranyaksha

Beat them back

To the dying plain . . . .

Under the Tree of Stars

They argued, Priest to Prince:

"Since the day before dawn,

I have foretold the youth and

Figuration of this Tree

Into your likeness, Prince;

Because I am an old child

And have been here before, often --

The perishing and the

Being born are one."

"What of the Adversary

In the dreadful wood?

What of the Worm

And Holder of the Rain?"

"Would you master him

With contingencies? --

Yourself and the drouth,

Armies compacted under

The balustrades of vision,

A rectilinear host unarmed --

Lion love in the tower
Of gazing, armed?"

"Passionate proud men
Hold the escarpments,
The bearded plain; hillmen,
For vengeance mostly? --
Of hill on valley,
Revenge of stone on stream,
Of Khan on Prince!

You who comprehend the whole
Without the parts,
What say you of all this blood?"

"I say, what is intended
Turns in the doing,
And the event strays far
And near with its own life.

Thought and accomplishment
Fail, fall, and move the zones --
Vast leakage of
Experiential time!

It moves by default
And is success.
Between success and you,
Prince of these Realms and
Outlaw whom the law adores,
Stands the white ape of Hope
With the archaic smile.

Who has the courage to despair?
Who has the strength to yield?"
"Teach me, my Cozener!"

(Now with the heart of beast
Encompassing my Lady,
Love fortifies her as he draws away.
She refurbishes her rayment with
Impetuous lineaments of love.)

They fought on the hills,
Barren slope, the
Wild storming horsemen.
Krishna the Prince
On the dry terraces encamped

135

With Baladev
Under the Adversary.

"The dawns go forth
To meet one whom the laughter
Of lightning bore,
Soul upon soul in one."

The lost into life
Bethought them,
Enquired the uses of
Weapons and death.
Strove the lowly striven.
Formed, hence the treason
In a dry land where
The corn is parched at birth.

"Lost in the black time
Of the year, these months,
Born with the human caul,
Drive down to soules deth,
Oblivion of men. . . . "

The Prince went up Rain

Mountain with Baladev.

Fiery by dawn were

The Serpent's scales,

Fiery by noon, he held

The water-hoard.

Hiranyaksha came down

Out of the forts,

An army of crones

Tittering in the rocks.

"O do not come

Close to the Worm,"

He said, "unless

You come in thirst

To pacify his hunger."

"That I must do,"

The Great Wierd said,

"And pacify you too.

Tell him: Let go the rain."

They fought for water and food.

The flashing dazzled them.

Veteran, Prince and Wierd

Fell back to the plain.

In the dry of morning

A locust young

Dragged its feet over

A dead cornstalk.

The Prince came to the Priest.

He said: "The charm I learned

From you did not suffice

On Rain Mountain. Will you

Rehearse your point of view

In other terms, or what

Will you take to offer twice

A grasp on my history?"

The Priest on the lotus smiled:

"There is no need for a Prince

To grasp: only that he wish.

Here I am, in your desire

To know me. Do not

Distract yourself with my history."

"Teach me, then.

There is but one rule --

That you be real."

"My presence here

Is an act of piety.

I can be real to you

Only as I become

Part of you and

You are part of me.

To become real we must

Use our imagination."

"There was a time, my guide,

When we saw eye to eye,

Your petty Prince and your Great Khan,

Kaliya your Dissident and

Baladev your loyal ---

Then all was real

As you and I."

"When the pure point

Of consciousness

Does not coincide with

The pure center of reality,

Eye to Eye,

One enters time.

When did your gaze first wander?"

"Events caught my eye,

Addressed me, and

Did not wait for my reply.

Now I pursue them

Far and wide."

"Give up, Prince, and go home!"

The assault again:

Again they fought;

Prince and Wierd

Fell back from the brighter sword

Of Hiranyaksha.

Kaliya's coils grew tight

On the water-hoard.

The people said:

"Prince, give over and

Anger them no more!"

The Priest said:

"Touching our Despot:

Do not be deceived

By mere evidence.

His outward or visible form

Is too consistent --

His personal shell

Seems stable to us

Because it does not flicker

Like our thoughts:

It tells us nothing,

My prince and hope --

That look of solidness is

The crowning trickery

With which we dupe ourself.

His next self is an apostasy

Of roving intellect,

An unreliable will.

So if you must, my changeling,

Look him in his diamond eye,

And fight.

During this spectacle,

Let Baladev pass under you,

Up Rain Mountain,

In a buried river-bed

Drier than our seeming drouth.

He will come out above you,

Above the forts that guard

The grip of the Pythoner.

Let him strike Kaliya's coils

And free the waters."

"I go," the Prince said,

"Into a perilous place.

There is but one danger --

That I shall not be myself:

Not that I may pretend? -- but

That I may not recognize:

I am the Prince."

"Imperilled and secure,

You are prepared,

Nothing can happen to you.

To me, the unprepared,

Nothing ---- yet

There is a wilderness

In which the peril

Is not imaginary;

For there is no one but you:

Catacombs in which

The worst anxieties

Are justified -- where

You will find

The skull of your goal, and

Hear the approaching footfall

Of your Foe.

These are as real

As you and I. And

There is a desert where

You are almost sure

To die of the drouth."

"Oh, reassure me!"

"How can I? But

There is a guide without

Whom Princes die,

Part by part, until

They are wholly dead.

Amor, go with him! -- But

Before the Wierd strikes

The coils on Rain Mountain,

Let him gain the Snake's consent!"

War devised then for

The cutting of the coils,

For the land's blood

Labored in lust

For the Sun Duke.

They sang him the poison song,

Outlander,

Arid master of want,

Savant!

"Baladev," the boy said,

"I and you shall go,

If you have the force,

Up Rain Mountain,

I to Hiranyaksha,

You to Kaliya's coils."

The Wierd replied:

"Let the rains come, and

The streams rifle our dust,

Tonight we encompass

The Encompasser."

To the Veterans:

"Equate in one stratagem

The forces of my argument,

Resolve them on

The precipitous hill --

War-lust will lap there.

The times of the Dissident I know.

Soul upon sand,

Tide-toppled proud one,

Hearken that lunar head!

Though you cohabit with

Your water-queans.

Prey to the twelve torments of matter,

145

You shall cry, Hear me! over

The rocks of the world!"

Underground,

Up a dry riverbed,

Baladev stalked,

Swordsman-wise,

On pollen sand.

Overhead the Prince.

They strode as one.

The princely guard

Fought Hiranyaksha;

Baladev came out

Above the forts --

Over him, cloud-massive,

The giant coils.

The Wierd said:

"I am Baladev.

Agree to this deed."

Formally, the great head:

"It is time."

The sword shimmered and thrust.

Lightning from it

Sawed the swollen sky.

Kaliya was the

Groaning of thunder.

Down Rain Mountain

The waters plunged,

State on state ,

Hungry loves

Had their will

On thirsty lands.

The Dead Woman arose,

A bronzed burgeoning.

Rivers: they bore along

The Worm's debris,

His men and forts,

The shields that were but scales.

The lucky Despot, saved

By night, called out

In flight: "Forgive,

Mansoul my Prince!"

But, "By degrees," the Prince said,

"In seven stages of regress."

Counsel, this from the depths

Of the River that passeth

Behind the eye.

No penman, that scribe and clerk. . . .

Disorderly drinking

Of all things -- the Prince

Ordered them: Peace.

Who would approach force now,

After such sessions?

Who had the taste for death?

The Priest said,

Governing again:

"Within the selfsame round

Of illusion, all of you stand,

Both young and rich.

Need you have moved?"

Adjusting their disputes,

He argued leniently. . . .

Mango, rice, tamarind

In the wavering fields,

Fish in every pond.

Beyond the mountains

Kaliya lay in death, but

Rising out of this death,

Grew watchfully back

Into the flood of time:

How many tides of man?

Million by that Realm reckoned,

By the horologer Priest,

Tracker of stars' intent,

Interpreting for the Prince,

A hundred hours only,

Though every seventh wave

Hove up a cycle of time.

Mist under the mountains,

A lake or a sea, flowing.

Veterans at the far passes

Guarded our Victory

From an estate of ghosts. . . .

Flame and flare at night,

That stayed in the hills.

Crimson, in the spoorless wild

Of the will, surging,

The eye of this will

Watched for the Worm.

Filming of incense to the Force,

Provider for the Veterans

Of pleasures that implicate.

A languid province

And the wild ones

Becalmed in sweet smoke --

How should the soldiery

Be unsatiable?

Baladev nightly fretted:

"Where are we Lords

And iron visitors?"

Then She to the Prince complained:

"What lunar scimitar

So debases Baladev

To domination of mere events?

What delta shadow
Dominates the Prince
With priestly looks?
O do you love me?"

That night She dreamed:
A day crumbled and fell
In glitters and bones:
Hiranyaksha in the Mirror Palace
A jeweled sword and her by the hand,
Touching her though She called
Krishna the Prince:

His answer, Despot, Prince,
And She: voices echoing
In a mirroring maze
Of corridors, unreal!

Multiple to a madness,
And a thousand cries
Mirrored in mirrors --
Which were the true selves?

Krishna the tender Prince

Brutally (the Khan's son),

One by one,

The iconoclast, testing,

Testing these forms, breaking,

Breaking glass echoes,

Fancies of Despots dared;

Looked for the one Lady.

With boot and sword

And cutting gaze he killed

Droves of brothering shades,

Bellowing mirrors, unanswerable

Arguments of glass.

Behind, the grand forms

Of Snake and Dog, of

Worm and Wierd,

Kaliya and Baladev,

Glooming and gleaming

In their strife of overlings; till

In this madness multiplied,

She rung and rendered:

"I am here, not there!"

By thirds the mirrors
Fell away, shattered in shards,
And the true Persons stood
As three. The raging Prince
Cut off a left hand of
The Despot -- o trailing
On the Dragon's arm he fled,
A faltering Lord,
Along the maze. . . .

"A snakish place," said Baladev again.
"See what a Worm has
Fattened on our rest.
He tightens around us and
Where is the Force we spent
On the peace we bought?"

Down from that pass then,
And the northwest princesses
Crying in a hurricane of
Horsemen o with glee
In their lances, Kaliya came --
A presence, a power,

A coiling doom, round and around,

Silent, reserved, unseen.

"All that is eastward," the Prince said,

"Where the Dragon's coils

Are most searching,

That way we may not survive."

"Westward," the Priest,

"Across a chasteness of death,

Lies your third province

And your last campaign

In the Provenance of Force.

There a Prophet's will

May strengthen your unwilling hand.

Here you have lost and found

Your seven districts in one province.

Here I instructed you in ways

To eschew unholy births

Without rancor. Remember also

The seven gross types of illusion."

The Prince said:

"I am ready to go, only

Let this Lady ride

Close beside me."

"Fat and thin

Are my men,"

The Great Wierd said,

"Hard to attach again,

Though I spur them over

Desert without end.

May they come to!

Flight is our fate

In the sun's wake.

After us will coil

The Noctule in his force,

Piqued to see Baladev,

Prince and all,

Escape so strong."

"Goodbye," the Prince said,

And the Priest replied:

"There is no need

To take a formal farewell.

Just go. Quietly.

Never mind making

An inventory of the

Things you are leaving.

Just leave them."

"There are a thousand

And one things ---"

"Goodbye, my friend. . . .

Now the world walks away.

I am alone with the world.

First, in the silent world,

Sitting still,

I dine on silence.

Then, in the silent world,

Am consumed in silence."

(iii)

Foundation of a song:

Flight of Force --

Rout of the conqueror

From unbroken places

Obscure and many,

To the Third Shire:

Bounded by rivers

And the advent in time

Of the long-footed women,

Their hair knotted:

Skipping like quail

Beside Grief River

Where the Prince must fall.

The Great Wierd said:

"I proceed indelicately

But with equal eyes --

For the visions of children

Are here untenable --

By defiles of

An unaccustomed land,

The marches thereof

And ourselves accompanied

By wandering smokes."

O presumption of

Equally weighed causes!

Out of the sand

Arose ever before us

The similitude of

A Hound, leading,

And of the Worm

Behind us, loitering.

Barren hills,

The dwellers with sharp aspect

Bearing arrows of

Fear and of desire.

Shapes of the flanking Foe,

Dune-haunting, to sinister hand.

Moon brimmed over the rout,

Forestalling them.

Tremulous cry and the

Parched throat at dawn.

They came to the first river;

Swerved northerly out of the trap. . . .

Facing from the far bank,

An army: fiery horsemen

On the sands, their

Lances neighing out

Over the waters.

Thirsting for a sacred river --

Vision of jealous archers

On mad horses

Piercing beasts and ourselves --

Under their eyes we

Ravaged the water

With our drinking;   bathed,

Purified us of

Recent sins.

Among them on the far bank

A swirl of white light

Around a soul-black beard,

The Prophet: "Stay,

Or if you come,

There is a test by force

Over these waters.

Who are you? For the

Reports are meager."

"Baladev," he said,

"And others;

But look again."

"O is it the Khan's son?"

"It is, though pale

From an inclement peace."

. . . . brought them across

Then with honors,

Fording the shallows.

The young Prince longed

For water and peace -- too soon!

We drew him back from that way.

Council on a sandy threshold,

Prophet in a swirl of robes,

Out of that haughty cave,

And Baladev:

"For the fierce Worm will come,"

The Duke said, "and you

Though fiery, will not be enough

To live, unless we

Mount guard with you."

Truce made, they rode forth

On the shapely earth:

Armed yet aloof, wings

Of a quadrant circle,

Hosts held, mists

As it were about a lamp,

Krishna the Prince

("Of the plumed war gear," they said,

"Presently ill at ease

With the Second Realm").

In the night of the first river,

In a far south satrapy,

The Python drank.

Army of two Realms,

Camel and elephant,

Horsemen and the footsoldier,

And Hiranyaksha.

Met there at noonday,

The Prophet's nephew said:

"Though I am disaffected,

I know your wile

If the rumors are true,

In shires to the east.

Here are like wrongs

To be reversed. . . ."

Kaliya:

"There is a duke,

Golden by sight,

A dog and strict,

Will conquer by

A golden perfidy,

Except for me."

So they conspired

While Veterans slept

In their habitual corpse.

Seven Lords kept watch

By a sick Prince.

(Lady, why do you wait?)

The bird sings with especial song

Before the Prince.

Out of a deep land,

Bearing their scrolls,

Word of desert crags,

Wells in the desert,

Poured into the astrolabe

Of the year-swept men.

Districts and divers nations,

Cities and satrapies

Brooded on Baladev

And the Rebel,

Let dark and light

Into the cavernous land,

Death into her fosses three

And all her zones.

Then the Prophet took horse,

Robes and the great mane

Of his horse flowing about him

Like an agitation of the soul. . . .

Strove, fighting by the river,

Baladev willing him on,

Duke of the dawn-well

Color of apricot,

Commiphora, of the white

Soul-blent dwelling.

That month a troop

Filed through the flaming winds,

Reached them: bushmen with

Roses, ravens, kangaroos;

Bearing tablets and omens

Down to the curly sea. . . .

Stonished by the whole army

At victuals under the tents,

Then leading the fettled

Mares with purple gums,

Roan, and hauling

Their own provender bran. . . .

Brought out the high dark-

Mouthed hounds (white!)

Leaping aloof like tall

Swirls of snow.

On the flank of the

Great Army stablished,

Their horses eating

White oats and barley,

Standing by the chariots

They waited for the crimson

Weather of the war. . . .

Furlongs shrill

With issue of goats and men

In the fulness of the year

Grew still, dying

With the dying Prince.

Ashen were the nights

Of Baladev when

Kaliya roved the borderlands

Of their joint sin

And visited their Prince.

Spider-perilous

The hours that bear you,

Cool Lady;

Not the sunny Prince

Alone in a shade,

Nor the dark

Moon-regent Kaliya the Foe,

Nor the glittering Despot

With the cramped hand; but

Your own tidal constancy.

Krishna lies thirsting

Where this Lady goes,

In the burning plain,

Between two rivers.

Robe color

Of all roses.

Kingfishers

Circling her,

O my Lady,

Why tears?

(Haloing her.

O my Lady

Why do you weep.)

"That flight!

What birds are those?"

Catfalls go arching down

The summits of the sun;

The stars find words

With which to warn

This blind Lady.

Servitors,

The lion-headed women,

Remote on terraced walls,

Make their shadows small;

Those on the periphery

Lean forward

Out of the taut gown.

The scrolls frown inwardly

From their old visages.

So all things warn

And tempt this deaf Lady.

New things are eager,

The old ones lean together,

Learned lion-forms,

In wooing of her

From her way.

167

She would not learn.

One night She lay

Composed in solemn sleep.

Red, red were the leaves

When She dreamed her dream.

Cringing She went

Down nightwood trails

Where every vine and vein

Delayed her for the brimming Foe.

Yet She escaped --

To dream that while She slept

Kaliya killed the Prince,

Tumbled the bloody blocks

Into the Third River

To float down to the Gulf;

That while She lay

In solemn sleep

The black torrent

Bore the singing head

Of Krishna the Prince

Gulfward and down;

So that She started up
Out of her sleep.
Through the unending night
She looked for the Prince.

Weeping She walked
Through a land of black
And moldy crops.
Heat and cold of the moon
Crushed the dwellers
In that shire.

Downstream She ran,
Came to the Gulf,
Went down and down
Beseeching the lost
And scattered body of
Krishna the Prince. . . .

O there in Earth Lake,
Deathheart's carrion core,
She was the weeping whore
Of the Great Foe.
When her corpse had

169

Sued his rage to rest,

She gathered up the

Limbs of Krishna

Into her ragged dress, and

Bearing them in her arms,

Journeyed night-eyed

Back through the boundaries

Of Nothingness and Chaos,

Death and Night,

Until She came to the place

Where the waters meet.

The Prophet stood

With a reed lamp there

And a smoky flame

That would burn as long

As the soul might stay

When death has come.

The Prophet said:

"In the dead of winter

A king is born,

The hoar frost routs

Late from early."

"Pity my load," she said,
"And crooked wit
That can not tell
Early from late --
But wait a little
Till I have done."

Quickly she worked
In the panic light.
With mud from the river
She joined together
The body's parts.

Mouth to mouth she
Forced the breath.
As the lamp died
The corpse of Krishna
Groaned to a birth.

First of all beasts
The finch spoke out:
"The Lover lives!"

171

Light rained again --
Our death-white crops
Sang up in green.

We clothed the wise
And veil-voiced Lady
By whom all creatures
Long to be adored.

°°°°°°°°°°°°

Migration to
The sea's edge. . . .
The Worm driven afar
Impoverished, exiled to
Insoluble shores of birth.

Descent of a sharp cloud　.
On the district that
Is last in Force borough.
(The light continues
With one tone,
Which is that of love.)
"There was a land,"
The Prophet said,

"In the Realm of Force

Between two floods --

But that is gone. . . .

You will remember

In the Realm of Water

When you hear the Song. . . .

THE PROVENANCE OF WATER

Up the Mountain
Through the jail of time
With seven doors
Each higher than
The one before,

Krishna the Prince
Stood graven and chained
To the concentric figure
Of Force,
The second element.

The Voice from the Water:
"Ascend the Third Level."
Krishna the Prince: "I, a branch
With a dry disease?"

"I am the mover
And the medium."
Krishna felt the

Fluency of movement.

The zealous Finch,
Pricking his thumb:
"Sir, hear the word
Of this wetness! He

Is your cause and cure.
Go up!" In rain,
In rivulet dipped,
He came to the Third Plane.

Vision of Water;
From her fluencies, Realms;
From her swelterings,
Estates and Forms.

A field full of folk
Rise up out of algae
At the water's edge,
Breeding, feinting,

Flare with old fire,
Slump down again

Into the Medium.

Third Day's vigil.

"What then? Sing out

All our strife

In the Third Realm!"

The Goldfinch on his hand

Sang out for him:

○○○○○○○○○○○

Yourself came over

The crafty sea, so eager,

To a working of new

Isles and isthmuses.

Mind's blue-white

Movement along shores. . . .

The Fleet rode

At anchor there.

In the shallow nests

Fled by them ever

Immutable floods;

Perilous passage,

Bringing a Lady
With eyes for the sea,
To a quick-souled people,
Iscandar their Duke.

On a promontory there,
Among olives and grapes,
In a clean town --
Jaladan and virginbyre --
The Khan's son
Set his courtly heart
A Third Realm, which is
The Provenance of Water.

After the long journey,
Fighting by sea. . . .
Suaging forth of gross tides,
Shoreline in metamorphosis.
"I am the world
You see as moon,
I am your center
As satellite.

The Scorpion lounges

On my Roof in Jaladan,

The North Star leans

Steadily against my door.

Pinning it till I come

Rolling in from the rocks.

(Sweet, it was good

Of you to wait.)

The Ocean, I, attacks;

I, Continent, defend.

Thrust between them

On my sand, I

My sentry tower stand,

In Jaladan

Prize of my war,

My wound and cure!"

Uphove the Rebel

Slow as clouds,

The Python's oldest kin

Dwarfed us on the skyline.

Hurl'd they then
Naturall elements
On these Lords ourselves
And interlopers.

We toppled them, we
Tucked them in timeless earth
Again in their bed
Of sulky sleep.

The Dissident we caged out
In the unlucky provinces --
O barbaries of
An east and Second Realm --

In Straitland
And Narrowtown.
The sun glanced from our gaze.
We lowered our eyes.

Gaiety of these Lords
Over the chasm where

The sea-borne Prince proclaimed

In Jaladan his virginbyre:

"This clear and

Wind-swept town

Shall be my shadowless dear

And guest of mind."

Forts on the stony coast,

Towers, sharpnesses and

Groves of the sea. . . .

A trim Fleet ferreted

Out from the ports --

Our own boys manned her.

Off Narrowtown

Kaliya caught them, and. . . . . . .

"One crystal word

From the Khan's son

To end this wantoning

And the whole War!"

"Then let Kaliya come

Here to Iscandar's town

And Baladev, to meet
Krishna the Prince."

We dallied prettily
With events!
Over the clear
And gale-scoured sea

They came, the Dissident
With double his demands
And the beaked birds
From Narrowtown. . . .

Treaty made
At their ease,
And dined on trust,
Dukes of the Realms,

Krishna the Prince,
Iscandar and She also;
We drank with the Rebel.
Not Baladev; for

"How can a Prince secede

From his own War," he said,

Or pacify as Kahn to be

And call it Peace?

O what is Narrowtown

To the Pythoner

Compared to the Realms

We left him, but a lair?"

Midnight with all at rest

But the drudging sea,

Sharply She cried out

In her boring bed.

Prince Krishna saw her

Haled away by night,

Her limbs alight, all

White plumes gesturing --

Flew after them and caught

By touch a swarthy cavalier

Knotted with him

In a grovelling fight.

Krishna felt

In his foot

The Snake's tooth,

Fell like a star.

"Treaty-mate or foe,

Kaliya my Pythoner

And Rebel friend --

Let her go!"

oooooooooooooooooooooooooo

ooooooooooo

By that slim ship outrun,

The Fleet milled in the Narrows.

Word came to them

Out of a jeering town:

"Krishna my Mansoul,

Grant me but three Realms,

She will come to you

With her usual honor."

oooooooooooooooooooooooo

●●●●●●●●●●●●●

Allies held
To their promises,
Out of a Third Realm
Her fires and watery demes

The Great Weird Baladev
Lured them, mauled them,
Mustered them down
To the breathing ships.

Your bright-eyed demesmen
Slid the landlocked shires
To landsend. . . . seagoing. . . .
Veterans hove down

Out of the mountain,
Facile as golden cats,
Bearing on their backs
Sequesterments of battle,

Set them for cargo
Terrible and biding
In the canebrakes,

Threw themselves

With wide arms
Into the waves;
Walked in the woods to
Invite the unforeseen.

Above whom will
The vulture fleer?
No, not these,
Predestined, fair and
Giant-limbed. . . .
Beside the welded sea
They harvest antagonists
As harvesters,

And the caravans
Of those urns
Have over them
A grateful eunuch.

°°°°°°°°°°°°°°°°°°°°°°°°°

Leaving the canopies

185

Of Iscandar, the serpent-struck

The unrequited Prince

Fared east uncured

In the wake

Of that Lady

With eyes

For the sea. . . .

ooooooooooooooo

ooooooo

Star by star

The impotent sky renewed,

Earth conceives

Her third impatience. . . .

The sea was onyx

In the mid-journey

And northward;

In the south, sapphire.

We started at sundown,

Oil flared on the waters,

Fiery staves
Lustered from the
Insoluble shore.

The paean rose!

° °

° ° ° ° ° ° ° ° °

Lubricity of leaves,
Of the sea's mane:
And the furling!

O race of leaves
Falling upon the
Race of water,
By the light
Of that level, by
The middle light!

The wind pulled us
Narrowtownward. . . . .
Tides that scour the sea
In grave cycle. . . . . .

187

John Berry

To bleach a musk

Or shroudy smell

(They said) or to cool

The coal in a sullen head

Strip him and strap him

To decks awash & with sun,

Let the wind love him

With water and salt,

The handling sea

Lave him, but

Let the cunning Leech

Have Krishna's wound!

Beloved of death

The poisoned Prince

Lay on deck in

The salt air.

With all his craft

And soldier's lore

The Great Leech probed,

Suckled and bled.

Brine, earth and air,
Time and fire,
These failed, all his drugs,
On Krishna's wound.

For this flaw
And Rebel's bite, no magic
Had Baladev, no guile,
No wile nor physic
For the pierced foot
Of the green boy
And the Khan's son,
The pythoned Prince!

Where was She
In his nightly need?
Walled in Narrowtown
And wailed away was her force.

Our ship fled through
The shamed air, the crew
Coughing amid braziers
Of dung and olibanum.

On Rack Island
We stranded him awhile
For the wise crone to mend,
That we might live.

The loved Prince
With the unloved wound
Saw the truth
Of our sick tears.

We sailed with our health
On the self-enamored sea
To sue the Pythoner
For his Lady.

Here on rock island
Wrappèd in morning fog,
Float the great, gray
Master-birds, the pelicans,

With the look
Of exiled statesmen.
They welcome the Prince

Of the pierced foot.

Through a flaw
Perfected early and late
Iscandar's dam
And Woman Leech

Diotima could send her shade
Among the friendly savages
Of Meagerland, and come again
With certain seeds.

Sorting them over on
Rack Island, beyond reason,
The Wise Crone
Encountered the Reason.

"At njght's fall
The gull-adopted ship
Is not more chary
Of her Abandoner

Than I of thee, nor
Prouder of her night,

Nor readier for wreck

Or wrong or day. . . . .

What sleepy boy are you?"

Nearing her cave

The dragging Prince

Heard her antic voice; and he:

"Drunk on Water,

A man to be, but

Dead in part, and

Nothing is known of me."

"The man you speak of

Is your key," she said.

"Here is your sandy pad and pallet,

Inside, near the door."

"Although I was referred to you,

Doctor, what I see here

Is so desolate and austere,

I hope only for death."

"Be neither hopeful nor afraid,

I am not pure; therefore, dear child,

I am rather widely known.

Corruption is my stock-in-trade."

"Each move bares me and I die,"

He said, "yet the problem of pain

Is not of my posing. If I

Could be still -- just once!"

"That is the move par excellence;

However," she replied,

"Contract no debts to darkness.

Let the pain go last."

"It is not, you understand,

That I would choose

At all costs not to suffer,"

As the wound defied

The apparent crone.

"So long as I

Am not the Khan,

Will this wound heal?

John Berry

Short of the Castle I
Shall be ill and partly mad --
Flaws to which
I am not insensible;

Were I an easy going Prince
Who never had known pain, would I
Make a move, would I incline
To ascend the Peacock Throne?

With such sharp tokens of his concern
The Great Khan attacks me.
A thorn or two may turn
In the giver's hand!

Daily the Khan provides me with
The wrong I need
To right myself and him too.
I can endure."

"Krishna, Rebel or Prince,
I could wish you more
Cogency for your years
If not for your manner of birth."

"Madam, your son may be
The Duke of this Realm
And you its emerita -- I am perforce
Egalitarian."

"I could ease you
With attitudes, boy,
But come awake
While I watch.

Let me look into
Your schism -- a
Most private pudicity? --
O what a vulgar wound!"

"Here the weakliest smile
Makes my wound grin,
The kites of pain unreel
And I fly again."

"Pain marks the spot,
Do not thoughtlessly erase
The indispensable symptom

Of your disease."

"Can your

More-than-medical eye

Plumb such a rift,

Practitioner?"

"I see where a Worm has been:

Abyss with seven realms in it

Split by seven chasms.

In this one Iscandar walks. . . . "

°°°°°°°°°°°°°°°°°°°°°°°

"The pain does not drive me

To distraction -- it makes me

Aware of my distraction,

It concentrates me.

Rankling and self-aware,

I mull on the Khan and source

Of all my suffering

Since my escape.

Fighting him wears me down

Toward a scared residue --

Garrison facing the painless dead:

To what end?"

"Here the quick must answer

To the quick, till they agree

On that which has agreed on them

From the beginning --

Surrounded by a cloud,

Wherein it is possessed

And unaware of things

As they present themselves --

Videlicet: your dawn shadow

On the cave wall -- rise up!"

"What is this forking root?"

"A snare that failed to catch a snake

Will trap itself

A shadowy Duke."

"I seem old and embarrassing

In this unlight, emerita."

"Love your shadow,
Lead him well.
He may be your
Guide in Hell."

°°°°°°°°°°°°°°°°°°°°°°°°°°

Baladev. . . . .
. . . . .craft innumerable. . . .

To herward we set course
In the wooden ships.
Deep-soiled countries,
Lake and Mere terrain,

Sending forth
Young men to do battle
For the daughter-in-law
Of the Great Khan.

Ships drawn
Like a bow
Up over the breakers,

Bulwark of the shore.

Siege to the fortress
On the edge of the sea
Where the Rebel
Lay with her,

The land drawn
About him, watchmen
On all the straits. . . .
Bronze shining

On the plain,
Voices of young men
Far from their native land,
Singing a rapid song.

On the carved shore the Rebel
Stared with horn eyes
On the crystal sea,
Unbending arms at his sides.

Plume of horsehair
Falconing -- foreign dukes

Fled back from that

Dismal leisure doom.

oooooooooooooooooooooo

"That this town

Should provide us with loves

Particular to ourselves,

Not recriminate

Nor wax heartless

At our hot felonies --

Done in darkness,

Questionable hour! -- for

We may not return

To dance on you again

Nor fire your beds

By a molten dawn,

Nor hunger in

Nor thirst with you

Under the crimson

Weather of the War."

Siege without a Prince!
Whose woman and war
Was it? Krishna's, yet
He would not come.
Ignorant walls unbreached,
Our lances faltering. . . .
. . . . marble virgin. . . .

°°°°°°°°°°°°°°°°°°°°°°°°

Bowmen from the back country
Know well
How to shoot down.
Still we presumed.

As the water lived,
So our men died.
Plague hovered us.
And the quarrels. . . .

Iscandar fished in the surf
As if for sport
While we fought on the plain,

No end in sight.

We can not carp at you, Baladev,

Because you are with us,

Shining one astride the

Fosses of our dead. . . .

Our strength marooned

On Rack Island

With the arid hag --

What pious rite moved you?

oooooooooooooooooooooo

ooooooooooooooo

Nightly centaurs came

Down for a fight,

Omens there of coming

And going, by day.

The big eyes of

The convalescent moon

Peer from the covers

At the nematode,

Fungus, nelumbo,

And the wild shining sorcerer

Migrained in

The world's mist.

Under the slain,

Under the crude,

Under the subtle dead,

Lies ritual earth.

Men standing like young elms,

Gigantic and violent,

Questioning dawn, gaze inland

Over the familiar battle-roads.

These wrinkles

Are from waiting,

Not from war. . . . .

Awaiting

The friend who comes

Bearing resolve,

That lance, for the

203

Long journey of a friendship,

The world is silent

As if it were alone.

In the night

All things

Delegate to the cry

Of a woman their cries.

He comes. The sun

Delivers us from thought.

Unprofitable death

Of men on the outer

Marches of the soul,

Far from their Prince.

On Rack Island

In the Realm of Water,

Fortressed without walls,

A crone and a prince debate.

Baladev: "Dig here

From these fosses

A ruled line back and

Down to the shore rocks

Near enough to this

Snakebyre and Pythonburg

To goad it without risk

Till I come again.

Do not provoke the Worm

With the language of events.

Tonight I sail back

For the unrecovered Prince."

. . . . slipped out by starlight

Into a red tide. . . . noctiluca

Tricked him to unblinking

Old eyes on the walls.

They burst on us with the sun --

Blinded, our trench undug --

The walls toward us glittering

Like a sea creature.

We shrank our lines

To the coast rocks; by the ships,

On sand, in foam, we stopped them.

Some of us stayed.

. . . . mocking us: "Spear them

In their element, fishermen,

As their young Duke spears

Tunnies with a dungfork!"

The city laid siege to us

Till their wheels and hooves

Sank in the sand too far. . . .

Our back to the snorting waves.

By night the darker form

Of Python reared

Over the calcined power

Of Narrowtown. . . . They lied!

Bantering iron on bronze,

Iscandar met him, fought

Not for her honor but for

The Childe she wed,

(O my Lady,

Why tears? . . . .

Kingfishers

Circling her.)

A pitch of night

We torched ablaze;

Our shy honor

Pierced their proud scales.

We routed them

Into the cavernous town.

The broad shadow passed

From us again.

○○○○○○○○○○○○○○○○○○○○○○○○

Dawn was a moonrise

Oared in a pallid ship

By weird and crone

Fetching our Prince.

We ran down the white beach

Into the breakers

All bellowing heart,

207

Cooed him to the tents!

When the Great Weird

Touched Krishna's wound

With Iscandar's spear

Burned by Kaliya's blood,

He drew forth

A furtive grub.

Force returned

To the Khan's son.

○○○○○○○○○○○○○○○○○○○○○○○○

We cracked the brooding

Mollusk of the straits

To tear from her

A solitary pearl.

. . . . breached them

At nightfall,

Broke in, into

The happy flood

Of fear and gold. . . .

And the persons --

How they tempted us,

So long withheld!

Free from these rites

The Great Weird ranged,

All justice in a sword, but

The Dissident declined

By night into his past

And Second Realm -- who

Could follow him

Into that cave?

With unfamiliar smile

She measured down to meet us

Out of his very nest.

We could not look at her.

Blinded, we saw.

The officious Duke tore from her

The beads and barbaries,

Put her on Gaya's ship.

Narrowtown laid waste,

Her capital goods

Weighing the gunnels

Of a whole Realm,

Her specie and jewels,

Scrolls and images,

And best, her persons

With their wills torn out. . . .

Caught the west wind

At ebb, and sailed.

Ship lies like a trout

In the quivering sea;

Passages of mass

Under-upon this

Long thing, this

Sliver, this

Dear ship

Constant fish!

She swims, she swims!

Cling to the finnies of

Your wriggling ship!

This is not water,

This is destiny.

Sundown, and :

Colloquy between

The Sun and Things.

If thou hast a mind,

Stay below,

At such an hour,

Ere night grab thy bow.

° °

There was a canopy

Upon Iscandar's deck

(Mansoul as amoret), with whom

Krishna convened. . . .

. . . some danger he might

Throw himself into the sea. . . .

"I am myself my own

Mirror and fist." .

Late in the year

For that passage.

Two days out of the straits

The first blow caught us.

. . . . new helmsman. . . .

Fought with a mess of gear,

The Duke as bosun, we

Lashed you to a mast. . . .

The Prince in chaos claimed to see

Through a clear winds-eye

The Castle, gale-scoured, and

High on a parapet

The Great Khan waved to him

As it were, Good morning Prince!

O then Krishna flared and

Flamed in his bonds:

"Now I'll encounter him --

To the Castle, Helmsman!"

"Though you are given
To accurate dreams,"

Your bosun, "First
Let us ride out this
Sensuous storm, and live.
Oh then we'll sail you."

"What wrecks us here also
Rages at the Seventh Stage --
All these storms are one!
Steer for the Castle!

We have come round again
In a cycle of wavering
To the magnetic pole and
Absolute from which I fled!"

But the vision skewed,
The night a netted lunatic,
Soul in shreds, and a wild
Prince awash on the mast.

Flotages at war on

John Berry

Water isthmuses,

Peninsulas of sea

Reared, roared down on us. . . .

That comrade, this friend

Gone overboard, the rest

Of us clenched to oars. . . .

ooooooooooooooooooooooo

Soul upon sand,

Tide-toppled proud one,

Prey to the twelve

Torments of matter,

Hearken that lunar head!

Though you cohabit with

Your water-queans,

You shall cry:

Hear me! over the

Rocks of the world. . . .

We who are with you

To the end----

Started at sundown.

Oil flared on the waters,

Fiery staves lustered

From the insoluble shore.

The sea was onyx

In the mid-journey

And northwards,

In the south, sapphire.

The god arose (you know it)

Like any desire,

Rapt us -- we

Hung there on the crest --

Immobile, death-defying

Delicacy --

Then. . . . .

Springs of fresh water,

Deer and wild grapes,

Cypresses, caves.

Why risk ourselves again

To blue and treacherous leagues?

Rested from
The long trip
And the War,
Counted comrades with us

And those not;
Fitted the beat ship
With a straight mast,
Caulked her.

"Is love new,
Or grief
Beyond life? Then
Why this languishing?"

Acedia,
Weariness at core
That cometh at noonday
Or a little thereafter. . . .

O star-tanned voyager
Discover to us

The honey
In our hollow ship!

The dawn girl
From the wave arose.
("They say the god
Wants us.")

We had not known
The broken stone would be
So fair. ("Has any god
Come to you?")

Trees like women's hands
And the souls of men. . . .
Three winds pass over
The race of leaves

That fell on the race
Of water. ("I feel
Wanted.". . . . "I also shuddered."
This rock is for Veterans.

ooooooooooooooooooooooo

217

○○○○○○○○○○○

Waves parted

Before us,

The mannered fleet

Stretching eastward

Over the sea like

The memory of a priest!

Venom gone

Back to his source,

Seas cured the Prince

And sight of isles.

Flower of brine

Of water and light

Of man·awake and

Blind with day,

The Doctor's heir

And ducal argonaut,

The long way round

Aged him again.

Out of old night

On tides of sun

From seed to stem

The green boy grew.

"You in the offing,

My flesh has flags in it,

My hair rebels,

Surely my breath is wrack --

I am not old enough!

Paler, wetter, weaker

Than seaweed in your tide,

I swim with you."

"If I kneel it will not be

To worship you more than myself --

I would offend by seeming not

To be one with you

Or seeming to think of you

As a Khan's son

Limited by

My separate existence.

Indeed I must offend

In being stirred by you

As by some particular thing

In which you flash --

Kind condescension

To your gross earthling!"

" I think this thinking

Threatens our unity."

"My consciousness is

The ultimate threat.

Only my death

Can satisfy your honor."

". . . . am not worthy

Of this noble race. . . .

. . . .will go forth. . . .

Solitude of a tree or cave,

Finish the grisly exploit,

Mean, without charity,

Love reversed by

The demand for love. . . .

. . . . return after death,

More general, presence

Felt then only as

A gracious affection."

"Mansoul my Prince

Of all our wounds,

Opening for whom

All things are opening,

Beyond the arcana of

Our special selves --

O realer than real! --

Walls reject you at their peril."

ooooooooooooooooooooooo

Hair-whitening isles

And icy littorals

Our ports of call,

By a swerving star. . . .

Again the Prince woke:

"In this untimely skew

And swale of time

Across a black flood

I sighted the high walls

On which my moving constant

Point of departure

Changelessly (we change) --

Paces: the Plural Man,

My Foe and Father, arch-enamigo,

As if he had not yet sired me!

Am I to present my case?"

∘∘∘∘∘∘∘∘∘∘∘∘∘∘∘∘∘∘∘∘∘∘∘∘

. . . . the Three

Who neither came nor went

But lounged like cats

In the Doorway to the Gulf.

"The wound was evil

But the visions were apt,"

The Prince said. "That was

222

For balance," Iscandar replied.

"What can be better than
Our symmetry in repose?"
"Victory," the Duke said,
"Victory is better

Than love or joy,
Better than harmony
In a clean Realm,
Or symmetry."

"I see no more visions,"
Krishna said, "but
What course is this,
Set northeast by north?"

"Homeward to Jaladan."
"Not to the Castle?"
"Prince, I do not speak
Of anterior things.

Court and the Games await you
On a foam-bound promontory,

The site of Victory

Your true home."

To leeward, the blue races.

Out of the wake, scenes,

Orderly turmoils and purities

Green white and the sun-gold

Crystals induplicable

But above all, movement:

Movement with the adoption

Of the moved.

In their sea bed rest

Sands of pearly bones.

Once they ached like us

From striving to be one.

Sands hold them down,

Seas pin down the shores,

Airs weigh on the seas --

What fiery word stirs them so?

°°°°°°°°°°°°°°°°°°°°°°°°

A sea snake in a fright
At our savage ship
Starts out of his element.
Wingless, he enters Air.

Archipelago to a month's end.
Isthmus. . . .
We coasted along the isles
To Jaladan.

"Sea-eldered Prince
Whom the wave detained,
Welcome to barbarous war
Not of our choosing, " Baladev,

"Sailing from Narrowtown
We took our ease, though
Not as you and he
Junketing till years end

Without your Lady. . . .
Ocean procured you
By storm. We were spared.

The offended sea --

Do I reproach the dead? --
The Manta-hovered wave
Informed your Foe and Pythoner.
Suddenly near, he struck.

Did we not humble him
At the far edge of the hook,
Across the watery drain
At your own docket and door?"

"Before night falls,"
Iscandar said, "I will count
This shell and pearly Realm
Of the Khan at Worldsend

By the Prince at hand,
In noble games, the
Blood and sea-gold pride of
The Provenance of Water!

The time is ungainly.
Muster your gracefullest,

Most clear, strong, and whole
For each contest.

Then let all those
Who aspire to Victory
Strive in good style,
Spirited though they be.

May they so far forget
Solicitous death and the War
That they have joy
And a good aspect.

Whoever by sword,
Intended word or plot
Breaks the truce
Or the tone of it

Shall start his wandering
After the last event.
No single Realm shall house him,
But the whole War."

They strove for Victory,

The best of them, gods,

In the Games of Darkness

And Force,

Earth and Air,

Fire and Light.

Do not begrudge Night

Its nobility.

To the Rebel went

Darkness and Force,

Water and Earth;

We conceded; but

We found in them

Our own distant stars.

To us and our Veterans,

Fire and Air and Light.

°°°°°°°°°°°°°°°°°°°°°°°°

Bitter the straits

Of passage

The Pythoner debates,

Bitter the dialogue.

Cruel year
Leading the young men abroad
With high hope of godhood
Found in battle;

White plume
Of the soul unfurled,
Marching into the
Crimson weather of the War.

Territory of
A blue-lipped wave,
Promontory foam-bound;
Truce made in the south

With the unsmiling rakes --
A Python's armory alive,
Who brought forth their young
Unpleasured except in strife --

They had a way
Of dazzling you

With their bare graces,

Then you received the shaft.

Pact sealed with the profile

Of the Khan -- betimes

Their mood being such, it may

Have been the Khan's son.

Forging of weapons, and

The badger hours

Harrowed the old men

Pacing the battlements. . . .

At the hot gates of dawn

Cramped on a chalky trail,

It seemed to us at the time

We were enough.

There we gave argument

To Death, all unknowing.

By reason of its girth,

It was untidy;

And otherwise presumed. . . .

Fleet guarding

The coastline against

A chained oar.

It may be as they said,

We refreshed ourselves

In the shade

Of those arrows.

°°°°°°°°°°°°°°°°°°°°°°°°

°°°°°°°°°°°°°

We fought well;

Fear made resolute

By desecrations and

The impure pomp of the stranger.

On the rocks,

With little speech,

We combed our glittering hair,

Gold or xanthous, gravely;

Seated there with our bodies,

Bode attack, loitered

231

For omens. Battle begun,

Glory mounted the day;

And the vine of the soul

Mounting also,

Over the barrows of

The morningland.

We garlanded the ground,

We two.

ooooooooooooooooooooooo

. . . . encamped on the plain

In full regard of

The Rebel past

And thunderhead,

Kaliya: we saw the gleam

Of him and would have

Grown weak but for

The Prince and Baladev,

Iscandar and the cool legions,

Our Veterans;

Along the shore

Our sea-raking fleet.

○○○○○○○○○○○○○○○○○○○○○

To us

Their ruses lacked wit

Or having guile,

No economy.

In their style

A profusion.

We taught them

Directness.

Caught, they cared little

For the smiling turn

Of a (thigh).

. . . . indirection.

The sky shimmers

With languor of silver bells

Laid waste.

Troublesome night grows near.

What shall be the deed
Of the dream-speaker
For the people
At such an hour?

Man of accomplishment
Easily crazed by sights;
Bird-winged neighbor of the gods;
Flying at the clash of bonds:

Pardon our guilty grins.
Make lasting songs for us
But remain with the very old,
The very young,

And the virgins,
Behind the walls;
For war disfurnishes
The imagination.

Having heard, go,
And let our deaths

Attractively appear

In the Event.

° °

Song, woven in the web of gratitude,

In the web of remonstrance,

In the web of a thousand

Reconciliations in war!

Sword of the new iron of Victory

Like the sickle of

The moon at morning

When She walks on the shore.

And the nobility

Of the men surpassing

The wing-tips of

The white sea-faring gulls.

O stone more clear

Than the blond eye of dawn!

And the Prince's thought,

Holding court

In the light-time,
Enters the commerce of
Soul's perilous terrain,
Night's bluntest edge.

Win or lose,
The Victory is yours,
Prince: you are
The opening of doors!

The beloved asleep
In the tent; vigilant
By the threshold
Is that other.

Seated beside his soul
He ponders
The earnest music
Of recollection:

A bloom of sense
Of sight of sound

Of daylight bursting
Into speech --

Hence these constellations
Of our intellect.
A Prince may question
The evident design.

How is the Child sleeping? --
Gita, lady of all
His thunderbolts, of
Grandeur, of the dance.

Archaic smile of
The white ape of love;
Stalagmites of passion,
In the cave.

In the flame consider:
Betrayal of the gentle spy,
Zealot of the bed;
And the beloved entrusted

To the folds of the tent.

And make secret promises

Of return to the

Mountains of essence.

O accomplishment of

Forgotten works,

Building of cities

In the wilderness!

ooooooooooooooooooooooooo

When the Sun has passed

Over our level,

Cities in the fidget

Of ambition

Are troubled for speech within.

Honor to the bearer of

Tidings of a land

Without honor!

Speak? The unspeakable hour

Rains, downfalls

On the silent laurel,

Scorning not

The previously ravished,

Words depart

With the announcement of

Limb-loosening night.

"Is it the wind

Blows your features askew,

Sweet sophist?"

"A nescience. . . ."

Whether we can apply ourselves

In the moment of waste,

To reclamation of

The Problem.

Holy people of

The western seas

Send forth colonies. . . .

Men who in the village

Danced much -- reared

By the mother's friend,

By the (well-) seeded word,

By water and oil. . . .

. . . . of the fair feet,

Body well wrought,

Born of a gentry

Ever unspotted by

A languor of marrow

That cometh late.

Bend the song also,

Swiftly. . . .

And the shores of the sea-journey

Stained with their huts.

Immorality of

The righteous man,

Head of the villages!

Foam of the distant wave,

Secretive undertow of freedom

On the cape of the scoundrel!

Foam! And the soul
With bright eyes is scattered
Over the sea-foam
Staining the journey's shores.

Bald striding hermaphrodite
On the wings of
Another species, lofty
And estranged and blind,

In the stretches of
The night, see
All things in
The shape of a few!

"The powerful do not change,
It is the weak
Who travel, strengthened
Beyond history."

ooooooooooooooooooooooo

. . . . the gross tide welds

With force of years

A brown and rocky land

To far allies --

Eloquent the sea-tongue

In the sea-cave; till

In a ferment of July

The field bristled

With grass and spears

Of the Dissident -- he marched

Up the land-neck

Where seas conspire.

Rebel with the strength

Of virgins and the condemned:

Bronze and armed with

Well-burnished bronze.

Cunning of arid men

On the soul's marches!

They fought bare

But to greet earth.

. . . . orations of

A great embassy and

Of a grown fleet,

The keels laid.

Krishna slept

At the inland rim of

Iscandar's domain

The crystal provenance --

Rising in farthest south

Muttering of bronze:

A narrowing of eyes

And of the will.

City laid plague and

The hewn tree undone.

On the hard-won demes

Of the sea,

Leagues of empire fell --

The far stretches.

Forboding of priestesses:

" . . . . . . sons of the like cities. . . . . "

By the long walls of Jaladan,
A town in shards
To the very hill,
Our promontory lost. . . .

Eclipse, and yet a Lady went
Once more to ransom
The birthright of the Sun
Beyond the moondoor.

Through a dripping wood,
The matrons chanting
The beast-song unkempt,
Lewdly she danced. . . .

Stranger of the forested slope,
Do you know
Of these marches where
The women cowl their meaning

In the voices of birds?
Moved, but with eyes
Of the whole body

Regard you?. . . .

ooooooooooooooooooooo

Zealot of the bed

Of young constraint, we have

Visited upon these cries,

Not crossed over.

The leopard disunited howls

In night's wood submerged.

Again the grown tide

Suages forth of the sea.

Arrival of one

Out of the fluted trees,

End of a willed voyage

From a windless isle:

Matriarch, who laid

In the Prince's hand

The hard root of

A star-bearing tree.

"More of yourself," she said.

Coniferous, odor of resin.

He remembered again

The sweet nut of pain.

In pride of thought erect

The rescued Sun above us

On the visage of the sands

Smoothed white and arid

The desert of the intellect

For the construction of

Circle, square, hexagon,

Numbers many and one. . . .

. . . . conflagration

Of the idea

Flaring over the

Marble of the day.

Brutal virgin

On the staircase

Of the Sun,

Steel serene,

Turn slowly,

Let the blue shield

Of your gaze

Mortice the wall of Being

With courage, prudence,

And contempt enduring,

For this transpicuous lymph,

This ghostliness.

At the dawn of night

Your intricate owl

Takes her flight,

Wings cutting the letter M.

° °

Still the Python grips

The Realm as satrapy

Where feathered Hiranyaksha

Breeds at will --

Our honor lodged

247

In a rude Court

Far by north remote,

We Veterans, we Lords.

Time by event we marched,

Baladev built us back,

Lashed us with his chagrin,

Charged us again:

Our geometer had ways

To square a phalanx

Or to velvet a squad

Down to a lion's paw.

Iscandar circled us

With spangles of strategy --

The Duke our pride,

Whom the Fourth Night wronged.

Formed in this fire,

The Prince behind us

And ourselves as omens, we

Marched down the dishonored plain.

We rolled back thunderheads.

Town by field the sky advanced

And stood on the Cape again --

How they had unmade it!

Though we engulfed our sea-bed town,

Where was the dawn heart

Of Iscandar's Realm?

Kaliya wreathed it in morningland.

We followed. . . . .

Forth over the sea

Of two lights, out of interest,

Love, and necessity.

The sun sufficient to itself

Molested us

In that noon land

Where the spring died.

Befriended by proud zealots,

Down from the Doom strove

We ever, the Sun inclined

At the shoulder of the stripling

Eastward, our faces set

Toward the Sundoor

Blithely at first and resolute.

We broke citadels.

Till the light left us,

Ill and old we came

To the well of night.

Still the Snake withdrew.

From our strife,

Boundaries and the

Desire of states;

From our harmony, death.

Armies fell to us

In the ultimatum of

A shrill horn and a cloud

Of colored shadows.

Thrusting them back

Into their own coils,

That was the long march.

We would not let each other die.

On the night road

We bore nations

On our lances, laughing

When they slept through us.

At Force River, far from

The wave-breaking Town, we paused --

The unburned counselled us,

The hesitant dead.

Fame clipped, shorn

Not by the wind-shears

But by ourselves.

The Three were unsatisfied.

Rasp of fall

In the passes when

The Python fell to us.

We pierced that world.

Who will conceive Mansoul,

By what star? Iscandar. . . . .

Many pale ones
Along that pool. . . . .

Krishna. . . . . . .

THE PROVENANCE OF EARTH

Stemmed he then
From his Third Level,
Krishna the Prince --
That of Water;

Until the Khan replied
Out of Earth:
"Now ascend
The Fourth Level."

"From this Water
Whereon I stand,
I sank or swam.
Now I know your Fear."

"You stand and swam,
Krishna my runaway.
I who was your Fear
Am your Heart."

In Krishna's hand

The goldfinch cried:

"Alarm! He is your Khan,

Lawyer and ground!

Krishna Chameleon,

Hear the hue of Earth

In all this soil,

And climb again!"

Krishna the runaway

Strove and stood forth.

Five streams

Fell from him

Marked the provinces

Of the Fourth Realm,

Zones of this level --

Vision of Earth:

Those things that anchored are

In solidness

And sue from it

By root and leaf or flower,

From Water to Air,

In secret keep of Light;

And beings that swear by Light,

In desert of mind, the homesteader.

"Sing out for me

My deeds, my bitter deeds

At the Fourth Level!"

The finch sang out for him:

o o o o o o o o o o o o o o o o o o o o o o o

o o o o o o o o o o o o o

Cloudrack, and the

Destinies of men

Herded through the far reaches

Of the journey --

Passing at midnight

Near the house

Of an old emotion --

Abandoning

Venery and dreams:

255

Bronze bell

Of the military, helm

And tactic of bronze,

Tongue of the Law!

. . . tribal coast, the

Wolf and the she-bear.

. . . . . fled to fight.

The land lay

Shapely before us

In a sea-curve   ·

Down the west,

Ripe as a vine

Into the south -- Medini! .

Bronze and peerless cock

With the tone of Earth!

Tarpaulin of

The beaked kings overthrown,

The Autochthon dispossessed --

How they were self-assured! --

Those who had not known

The equable Law, we pardoned.

The true Rebel did not

Come again to Medini.

In a mixed country

Law is the brazier, therefore

We did not show rancor --

Were they not lax enough?

Republic set on the stone

Of our resolve (Arjun!),

Here we gave Earth again

To the Khan.

In the largesse of morningtide,

Into the greater sea,

To the brown estuary

She came, tremulous and sullen.

"A rough city and

Not my pearly town,"

She says, "So I make shift

With magnificence?"

257

Shadow of all our fire,

The Cheating Child

Who so cozened us.

(Kingfishers circling her.

O my Lady, why tears?)

Reunion in a false and

Winding dawn -- Prince,

You slept a darkening sleep!

Medini her jewelled moat,

Her Court the Capitol,

On the gates of noon

The cock as eagle crew.

○○○○○○○○○○○○○○○○○○○○○○○○

Tributaries from the blood of

Ten thousand tribes

Enfranchised; the Law

Made perfect.

Treaties signed

With ambiguous boors,

Arjuna Beak-o'-Bronze

Marched down the long shires;

High-riding plume

Of the cock,

Aloft and kindly cruel

To a toadying world.

We stamped your face upon

The grave northern main,

The weary-born, the

Python-suckled south --

Littoral more poignant

With the palm

Than the recovery

Of ancient cities!

We singed the sere rim

Of a continent

With the blood of

The Rebel.

Where a town
Of consequence,
Interrogating our beasts,
Found sin.

Medini was Earth
Wide with Water and Force
When the Snake recoiled
To the Third Realm.

Drained of its Force,
It fell to him, and
What was it but a shell
On a shore of alkali?

By a harrowing tale
Over the painted sea
Iscandar came late
As dawn to Medini.

Hermiting in a shell
Of Jaladan, Kaliya brooded
Over the sea
Of two lights.

Daily the Great Wierd

Hounded him

Over that lake and

Nightly by land.

. . . . took these provinces.

The geese. . . .

. . . . north and west,

Wintered south.

Conspiracy of

A long night:

Far borders and

A grinning foe. . . .

Bodies of men

Sold at the fair,

Still they move;

Of women and beasts also.

World between them,

A lordly shadow night,

Who but the Pythoner

John Berry

Brought Iscandar here!

A slave of ruses,

Talented to obsess.

Krishna perceives

Omens about him:

"Why did you not come

Like this before?"

Though Baladev proclaimed:

"Let all slaves go."

"Trust me," the Prince said,

"Do you think it takes

No courage to hold him

Here as I do?"

Word arcane

Where stars conspire,

Loves kingdome circling

Before its time.

To the august places

Come ignorant men,

In the blue stare,

Promise of thunder

Of alien ways

Beside the times

Brought forth in guilt,

Our weary noon light.

"Justice and Law

Prevent them," Krishna replied,

"Thankfulness

Hems them in. . . .

°°°°°°°°°°°°°°°°°°°°°°°

O love which is

My absolute alas!

I am lonelier

Than the Khan!

I who went into the world

Thought to rise

Out of my terminal,

Rocket out of

263

The resourceful shall

To one gasp of nothing

That I have seen or been;

That should not be humid;

Above the mud huts

And the house-tops!

Efficacy of counting time

Only by summer and winter solstice;

And there would be

No laughter that comes

From the tributaries

Of mirth. . . . . .

Lips that know not

What they kiss --

Lips of fish

Kissing their medium. . . . . .

Here the leaves die

But do not fall.

I who once listened well

To the soliloquy of a savage tree!

Nothing human

That is not alien

To me in Medini.

Rather let us turn. . . .

Grieving with sick eyes

Over the pages

Of the world

I would have made --

Transmutations

Neither false

Nor slavish

To the old text

But as lewed love

Independent of misdeeds

Whether of crime or virtue,

A selfless thing. . . .

Without advancement

Style or recompense

(I) have made the façade

Of a hill journey;

Countenanced

Going and coming;

Because I dreamed of

A hall beyond furtherness

Where heroes, gods

And genius converse

In democratic peace,

Witty and phlegmatic.

A barren busyness

My Court and Capitol,

Eyes continually averted."

Look behind you, Medini!

The faces of Kaliya do not forbid.

Shadows of wolves

Command the hunters

In the dry leaves.

More than stony Arjun

At days end, more than

Iscandar Victor and Baladev --

Not more than She nor the War

Yet more knowingly,

The Culprit came to the Prince;

In rags of seersucker.

We built the Serpent Tower.

°°°°°°°°°°°°°°°°°°°°°°°°

They said of this Lady reading

In her gold writing room

And her gold palace, that

Her friends squandered her,

For She had magnificence

Visual as the wicked Prince

But was herself unseen

Amid evidence.

Omniscient of names,

Of names of names

Of Love which is

Her absolute alas! --

The oblong deserts of

Her studious lamps

Covered the desert

In concentric webs.

Two loves lay thus

Before the doubtful tower,

Wherein sequestered they observe

The demon flaming in the bush.

Over a mountain range

Near by northeast

A pale foreshadowing of light

Draws like a seine

Out of the morningland,

Prizing a solitary star.

What sphere tempts the Worm

Out of the Green Prince?

Simple beginning, hard to end!

It was no more than a lordly clown

Like your diurnal man

A mere outsider with a lute.

A song in seven notes

Dawned from him as one,

Excessive but unique,

Light or Amor.

Familiar but solemn as

The Laws of the Blood,

Of the Backbone, and of

The Tree of Nerves.

Whoever heard that song,

Though eaten and marched upon,

Trembled to find himself unknown,

A spinster; and he conceived.

Those whom men make glad,

Lovers of womankind,

The slim who pass between

(Though not with impunity) --

Hearts began to stir

269

In public images long effaced
Or lost under their fame.
Fluids washed them, love moved them.

Trees called aloud
And shook their branches,
Walked from far shires
On their roots by moonlight.

Wild beasts on tiptoe came,
Stilling their lust, and sat about --
Merely to listen was to be
At once posed and solved.

Cautiously the lunar stones
Came wobbling up,
Freed of their curse,
By fiery life impelled.

Wind lay down with the wave
On a listening shore.
Rivers gathered and
Held their breath.

In city in wood they heard
That lute and fatal song
And stopped all their undoing
For seven notes or one.

It was no remedy for jade
Nor wings for the graceless cock,
But rather a mere transparency
In the Provenance of Earth.

"O now we know," they said,
"The towering Prince
Is not our own although
He was the Khan's son born!"

So they refused
Their past and vulgar luck
And were intolerant of all
But that intolerant minstrelsy.

The reeling Pythoner
Heard their descant -- O
Were his deviate powers enough,
His trial come anyhow?

(What metal tempts the Rebel so,

But his own gold

Hid by himself a battle ago

Under his threshold?)

Brass, drums, nails

And rival lutes scarletly jigging

Kaliya called out to unform

The regal night.

For the gangrened boy,

"Gong up delicacies

More virginal and barely born

Than once he was!

Dance your deaf Prince

Through circuses of sense.

Only when he has drowned in sleep

Will the danger pass."

At midnight through the barrier sound

Kaliya went to find

The Jongleur where he lay

Under an olive tree to sleep,

Realms tucked round him,
Empire over his feet.
"Minstrel," softly by starlight
He said, "are you alone?"

"Always, Kaliya, among
The destinies and dominances."
The Dissident replied:
"In the Seven Realms

Each power has a meaning,
Each meaning a shadow
And each shadow a power
Which you cannot have known

Among the orders, for the work
Has left you and works upon its own.
Can you submit yourself
To the aggregate?"

"Into these meanings, these shadows,
These powers, the Prince came.

Through them I go,

Though it cost everything."

"For clown or khan, Jongleur,

The rules of the game are hard.

The young prince has made them

To cost everything,

Whether you break them

Or abide by them.

You cannot coerce him,

Cannot reveal yourself --

That were unethical,

Permitted only to me.

Indeed you took a

Liberty in coming."

"My place is not limited,"

The Minstrel said.

"Granted" (the Dissident),

"Therefore, to guard against

The passion that made

Of the First Realm

Your drowned captive,

Let us consider the odds."

"What separates us but

A subtle, absolute nuance? --

You parallel me, Dissident,

In the Autochthonous mode.

The rules were more lenient

In the beginning.

By and large, I have

Conformed to a deepening game. . . .

Are you instructing me

In the arts of a gentleman?"

"Oh Lord, Sir Jongleur,

I am not of that mode!"

"I will not change

The elements of Air,

Of Force or Darkness,

Water, Earth or Fire;

And if I reach Light,

The whole War is mine.

I will not change you,

Essential Worm."

"Even to guard his health,

On which yours is contingent?"

"And what of yours?

The equation stands.

Agree: We are subject to

What a mixed Prince (born strangely, though,

Of both honor and fire) may do

On an off season, in a muddy Realm!"

"Alas," the Worm said,

"Nothing is more easier

Than to outwit a gentleman,

I proceed in good faith!"

In the starlight,

Under the olive tree

The Minstrel laughed,

And all the leaves tittered,

The stars shrieked from afar,
The far sun roared and the blue
Lute struck a chord
That stilled the whole War

From nearest, deepest dark
To high beyond and light as light.
On then the Song began
On the word *Amor*.

Stopping his ears, balance gone,
Kaliya leaped the roundelay
Of stones & sauntering trees,
Pavane of fowls & reel of beasts

Till he had come in flight
To the towering Court
And the Court in the Tower
Awake, lulled to the quick.

Rubbing their eyes already wild:
"We heard three notes
That take us back in time and zone

To the prewar panzodion."

"O chase those three notes

Out of mind before sunrise --

They doomed the First Realm,

So they may doom the Fourth!"

By waning starlight,

To the dash of gong, darkly

The deaf arrest the Minstrel

In the song. . . . . . .

oooooooooooooooooooooo

"What was that hammering?"

The Prince inquires.

"It woke me from a most

Perilous dream. . . . .

Now I am awake, why

Do I not begin

My daily convalescence

From sleep's ravages?

My rest is plagued
By famine, fired by war.
Waking, I am fearfully
Born, and die -- but

Why was I not told
Of Death's coyness?
My symptom is perhaps
Best described as Alarm.

I have awakened to
No higher a level
Than existence.
I have not escaped

The filtered world
Of symbol and apparition.
Oh, the dream world
Was child's play

Compared to
The Provenance of Earth!
That hammering! It is
Everywhere --

John Berry

Even where
I am not listening!
Can it be
Some one's heart?"

oooooooooooooooooooooooo

"Welcome, recluse," they wreathed
When She came to the tower
With her courage and fear
To speak to the Prince only.

"Auguries prefer a nightmare
Worse than any before," She said.
"I heard the song I dreamed
In the Provenance of Force.

. . . . . I and you
So presently are given
To the dear key-cage
Of our daintiness,

Memory deceives

280

The look of things --

Let the Minstrel go

Back to the First Realm. "

The Prince said: "No.

The song has no sense,

Nor do I hear it

As you seem to claim.

The Minstrel comes to me

Vengefully and surely

From the Great Khan

To sing down the sun!"

° °

Thus was the Jongleur

Who would not bend the song

To the Realm of Earth

Nailed to the hickory tree.

On the first night

The song sank down into the

Deeply wintering roots

281

And farther still,

To where conflict is pure
Uninterrupted repartee
Between flame and the soul.
One note, and the dancers froze.

Those among them who, caught
Unawares, heard through and through,
Dropped the embroilment
For a wintery flight.

On the second day
The song mounted up,
Leaves appeared on the tree,
Whirled away on the wind,

Into the provenances,
Zones, shires and galaxies

Of the Khan's Empire
To the sevenmost Abyss.

On the third day

White scented sails --

O flowers of centuries

Opened upon the tree,

Fell into the river and

From Medini they embarked,

Were carried, sailed beyond

The Gold and the Black Gulf.

Where was the hanged man

Whom they came to burn

Peacefully on the tree?

All stood as before.

In the air departingly

They heard the echo of

The lute and of the song

Beginning with the word, *Amor*.

ooooooooooooooooooooooo

oooooooooooo

Nail of each man

Starred in the firmament

Begun at skin's edge:

O what kindled ablaze

Souls on the delta of

A great termination?

Word-bearing wind

Out of the Realm of Force.

Solar voice,

Translator of the Prince,

Begin at the beginning

Where we began:

By the brittle gates

And needles of despair;

By angles of windows,

By the accumulation of walls;

By the tombs, by the

Shuttle of all thoughts

Over the loneliness

Of time, Jongleur! -- you came.

We who had thought ourselves

Used, were void merely --
Miracles of virginity!
You pierced us.

What to the Rebel was absurd,
Our honeymoon -- until you
Left us windowed here
In our own tower.

How shall the wit endeavor,
The heart once bent on venery
Burgeon in this bony ground,
Or the ground respond?

°°°°°°°°°°°°°°°°°°°°°°°°

"If I am caged in
My own heart tonight,
Why then does beauty
Give me no delight?"

Bitternesses blow
Over the Prince,
Changing his color,

285

Form and rumored game.

"My heart is filled
With its own reasonings,
Perfect, impenetrable.
Thou canst not enter!"

"I will break thy heart."
As horribly as lifting the world:
Eerily as a bee; painlessly
As the folding of a joint.

"Thou who dost rend me
Dividing mine from thine,
Send me forth from my court-house
Vanishing. Enter thou in."

When the heart is
Broken upon the rack
Of things that are,
Then there is black and light;

So that the Prince
Secludes himself in deserts,

And the fasting there

Causes the bones to dry,

Reins, liver and lungs

To know chagrin.

The meaning

Of his meaning,

That is Amor,

Remains to knock

Upon his

Fossil door.

°°°°°°°°°°°°°°°°°°°°°°°°

Wrath of a headless Realm

For the wronged Khan!

The Wierd found criminals

In the provinces

While the Litigant Worm

Won a stay -- Kaliya

By his black eidolons

In Medini. (Thence

287

Mounting nightly on

The rind of the world,

By his swart armies coiled,

He grew again.)

Citadel. . . . .

Choice of servitudes,

And the attrititions of liberty.

"Must I then?"

"Thou art for that."

Flower Town. . . . .

City in

A White Flower!

THE PROVENANCE OF AIR

Darkened by Force and drowned,
Entombed in Earth,
At the Fourth Level lay
The moldering Sun,

When out of this Air
The Voice came: "Rise
Three times more!"
And he: "What am I but

A coal, a moldering clod?"
"Krishna," the voice said, "Krishna,
I am your breath. Ascend
From Earth to the Fifth Level."

"Prince," his chirping finch,
"The Light shall be
Comprehended through
The doctrine of Air!

Let Air be not disregarded!"

The Prince rose up

Into the Provenance of Air

And breathed;

But oh! what

Nakedness was there

At the Fifth Level!

How clear the Vision was !

Birds whirling

In the green of dawn

Design the double

Flanges of a wheel

Over an olive tree

Wherein were nails.

The goldfinch said,

"Here I began to fly,

Where all true things

Are thoughtful."

"Sing out their qualities!"

The finch sang out for him:

When in that autumn

Of the pallid leaf

The Ghost began to sing

And Love to whine,

Then the grave

Equitable morning summoned

Him to move on or

Suffer that arrest.

The Black Current

Of the Dissident

And his own guilt

Drowned him in Earthen Lake.

O in his cradle sheet

The print of the Jongleur

And three hairs of

The Dead Man lay! --

Who came as one

Invented fully grown

To the Fourth Level,

Was awakened by

Thorns in his feet

As he stood under stars

On our prairie,

In our savage wood.

(Mountaining they sojourn

By a leaded sky where

Pythoners rebel and

Princes come to die.)

°°°°°°°°°°°°°°°°°°°°°°°°

"The heart of infirmity

Shall behold the heart

Of eternal health,

The Liar compelled to be

A kernel of truth,

Vision within a vision,

Planted in the most

Favored humus of time.

Dark diver behind

The celadon gaze,

Behind the glaze a veil,

Abstract or near,

Behind the veil

A river passing by;

Whereon a White Lotus

Swims. Here dive.

°°°°°°°°°°°°°°°°°°°°°°°

Through that stroke

Which heightens consciousness,

You rising out of

Your bed of roots,

Regardless of design,

Time or environment

May without precedent

And suddenly, Prince,

Cut across process to

The journeying absolute,

Yet do not escape

Your trial, Realm by Realm.

293

"By khan and lute,
By finch and flower,
When this Jongleur
Stands at the core of me,

Then I am no more
Your popular pawn,
Nor knight of my
Own idiosyncrasy!"

In the eye a cave,
And in the cave
Darkness of midgard,
Night of the guilty mind.

To the said byre of
Your anonymous man
Beasts came and all
Naturall things to see

The straw bed of
Your lean and troubled Prince.
Acorns he had and water

And bread he gave.

Bears and wolves,

To pardon you their wounds;

A stag also, formal

But for the eyes;

All manner of birds,

Besides your finch;

Begged him to take back

The uncivil dole.

Still you would not

See us as ourselves

Nor Realm as Realm

Nor Foe as Foe.

As postulates of guilt

And souvenirs of grace,

Prince we could not

Take our ease.

Among the animals

There is a law,

That each must represent

What is meant.

We who had not left

The prewar panzodion,

Were not partial to

Your Grand Tour.

○○○○○○○○○○○○○○○○○○○○○○○

Canticles of

A geomantic moon

Filled him with news

Of loves eternitie.

Night of stars

A pear tree blossoming,

Dill green the egg of light

That holds the day.

Frail green the jail of light

That held the sun,

Frail the pear tree

Where the stars were hung.

So rode the beggarly Prince
In Jonglerie,
And She, intuitive,
Urged him with dreams.

° °

The Duke Narada:
"Water the White Flower
Each day with one
Of these lively tears,

Till Gita comes back
To the end of a thousandyear
With word of Worldsend
And what She will find there."

. . . . to Arjuna that murky phial
Of crystal monadologies;
Rode out by morning
With the Prince and Lady.

° °

Out of the Citadel

And the Flower already stone:

"A moving pallor

As of the inclement moon,"

The Prince to Her,

"Betrays your flower-vigil;

But this Duke, born

With hearkening eyes,

Has the visage cured

In three climes.

Will not all this change

On our pilgrimage?"

Northward by north,

A deep descending wood,

Misled by starlight

And the motley Worm,

Through copse and cwm

Of that ungainly Realm,

Down the days edge

To the Ditch they came.

Beyond security
Of tears or rage,
From their dark compass
Gita stole or strayed.

"She goes alone," said Narada,
"When solitude is pure;
When merely strong,
With us."

They called Her through
The grieved and wrack-webbed Air.
Closer than mist,
She went preceding them.

Inches were centuries,
For She went deaf.
"Here motions fail,"
The Duke said, "and the will

Is silent, yet is
Frequently re-burned.

Here even the weak

Are malcontent."

"I have come here before,"

The Prince said,

"But the sequence and

The forms are turned."

The Duke said to him

As they went down:

"Regarding your question

At the time we met,

By which you seemed

To show wonder at

The erosion which

My face betrays:

It began true

As eros to lay waste

And at one and the

Same time to be,

Both within and

Without my visage,

Cured first in this clime

Which we now enter."

The Prince said:

"Was it the Second Realm

I burned or had burned,

When all was transitive?

Although at my rope's end

And the Realm's,

I knew well the

Extravagant abyss,

In this body I

Have not been through,

And am of no temper now

For the fire.

She once went through for me,

Who goes for herself

And with a soul sophisticate

To these flames. . . ."

301

"Prince, this is the route
Of what precedes you."
So then through the
Cavernous wood, whereof

The trees were flames;
And standing in each flame,
A singular soul,
At the theme of its sin.

ooooooooooooooooooooooo

Rose like a girl in tears,
Hair nonpareil,
Combed for you Veterans,
Nubile that day!

"Has a Lady come this way?"
And the trees,
Flaring their flames
Now and more white,

Leveled their burning boughs
At the path ahead.

"Through what marvel
Has She come through you?"

And they to him echoing:
"Through you!"
Those words, though ghostly,
Burned of a gold

Alchemy in his breast,
So that the fire
Which was so aloof,
Already swerved and entered

At his behest and
Murmured at its work,
Steadily consuming
The live ash:

"This human voice
If I reject, this rust,
Effluvium from the
Decay of stone,

Mold, oracle

Or squeak of rot,

Excrescence by which

The inner Strife is known,

This fine gas of

Consonants and vowels,

Then I reject Air,

Where Light feeds, and am not!"

With live eyes

Accurately singling out

Each and all of

The many colleagues

Whom he had thought to leave

In stabler Realms,

The questioned Prince enquired:

"Why are you here?

From love of the Worm

Who so bedevilled me?"

And they replied: "No,

From love of you."

"Oh, then is it exactly

The same?" that Prince.

"The flame is the same,"

They said, "though less pure."

From that word he quailed

And thrust himself

Into the hottest flame:

"Let me stay here!"

But "No!" this friend

Hollowed itself around him

Like a rosy lotus

And called out:

"What new flaw is this!

Is there no fort

Safe from the perverse bee,

Either in cities

Or catalogued in

The meditating flames?"

The Duke, smiling a little

Pulled him on,

For, "This is one of
The temptations," he said,
And, "How like old hickory
Your face is."

oooooooooooooooooooooo

Beyond the crisp ravine,
Krishna remarked:
"I thought my senses
Recognized in the fires

The lineaments
And crackling idioms of
Persons whose love I
Could not but return;

And also certain
Abstract countenances
Of those that look
Fated to involve me."

The Duke replied,

Painting back with his finger

On the sooty air

Whence they had come:

"All relevant ones are here,

Trial for trial, shire by zone,

Each in his own theme,

Bound by his desire

To the flame that pertains.

They deal with deep flaws

That opened once

Under your command."

"Here I stay!" the Prince said;

But Narada: "Sire,

I would not lightly choose

The sabbatical.

Royalty being, as it were --

Insofar as it is itself --

Absolute, is not spared

Infinity; whereas

This place is all ends,

A virtue for private men.

Even your deaf Lady

Has gone on ahead."

From provinces,

Great hollow-throated singers,

Song-brained, zelotic

Darksters, many exiles from

The Dissident (far-striking

In the dreamweeds),

For whom your fairer loves

Were burned last year.

"These gave great gifts

To the miserable rich,

Too late. Beware.

Impugn them and pass on."

Still the Prince delayed:

"If I am not in error,

There are those here

Whose valor in the War

Is, as it were,

A light conspicuously white,

To which the personal

Flames cannot aspire.

I perceive there

The fiery habit of

My Veterans charred

In four disasters."

The Duke said: "Here one may

Distinguish fire from flame,

As one would causative principle

From the substantial agent.

Think on the gamic flame

You so violated, as male --

The scene connubial.

Have you not taken the thrust?

° °

They follow you

309

Provided you do not

Retrace your steps.

Their responsiveness

Is so refined in the flames,

That they hear from afar,

Beyond us, and obey

Three notes of a lute.

She who precedes us,

After whom we go,

Lags for us up this

Stubborn steep ground.

Between this end

And this beginning

It would be well to move,

In present truancy."

Obedient to the

Informed causality,

Led and leading

The emigrating flames,

Krishna climbed, yet
His gaze knifed back
And down, to see
What personages darkened

As they, forming,
Rose up the cool hill.
With his left hand
He warmed his frosty throat.

Halfway up, the Duke warned:
"Steady your thought
Before each step or misstep.
The trail has changed.

When the Minstrel passed,
Rocks we might have used
Rolled elsewhere, leaving
This laminated shale."

Leaning, the Prince
Motioned with his hand
To those below, who
Sank down like a flock

Of rooks that has been
Molested at night
And fluttering to the
First unsocial place,

Gapes about and waits
For the sun's advice.
"But why is there no
Soughing among them?

Seldom have I heard,"
The Prince said,
"A more complete silence
In a throng!"

"Matured for the present
Season by the flames,
And this briny coolness,
They meditate," The Duke said,

"On their relief,
As soldiers seldom do.
Three orders freed them:

The Minstrel, She, you.

Now watch your step

On this precipitous path --

Worse than none, yet

The best conceivable:

It leads out of here.

Believe and bear it!

If you believe your gait

Could bear more speed

Without imprecision,

Then look up there --

Cautiously -- where

The rocks are confused."

Raising his eyes to

Where the sky declined

Over the stone-crowned,

Stark and toilsome peak,

Remotely the Prince saw

One who paused and climbed;

Then he called out in

A voice that echoed loud

In that silence, but

Was She not stone deaf?

Hesitantly She turned,

With the slow aspect

And pallor of one

Who is loth to look away

From a horizon; till

His view blurred.

Her right hand lifted itself

A little, and waved

In echo to his waving,

Then She sat down

As if tired of hope.

"Is She not beckoning me?"

He asked. "By her airiness

Home itself must be near!"

Duke Narada said:

"Shouting is not usual here.

Now you can feel

The silent twittering,

Some flaming anew,

While others rove.

I must descend once more

To rectify (if I can)

The unseemly gambados

Which cause such raggedness

In the ranks of

The newly virginal."

The sharpest third

And perilous summit

Of that declivity

A Gymnast scaled,

So spirited was he

And so light

After the tropic past.

Smiling, She returned

Some few threading steps:
"With your heart's heat
I hear once more. Prince,
Will they not think us friends?"

° °

Helping each other climb,
By stone and ice,
Up the last and most
Precipitous face,

They came in darkness
To the cold hilltop.
There, wrapped in his cloak,
They were cold and warm.

. . . . thrones fierce and occult
By the black winds ignored.
. . . . spoke of fires felt,
A time to see.

"Love, aeronaut,
I hear singing ashes!

Bodymaster, your
Ashes are a-song!

For long I put Love
From my heart, Lady,
Until my soul was clouded;
But then the bolt

Walked down through my heart,
And Amor entered
As between curtains,
Pushing the halves apart."

On Half-Dome Hill,
By Windy Peak, the dawn
Woke them with unnatural
Rainbow clouds,

Splendors abalone
And looking-glass.
"These shivering colors
Welcome us to the Air,"

The Prince said, and

317

Looked down: "O is it death?"

Three steps more -- a

Fall of Nothingness!

From the Abyss

Lichen flinched away

Blanching, to press

A grey face into the rock.

Who was there

But the black winds to warn

If in the night

A minstrel came this way

Or a prince in passing

Or a tired lady?

Three more steps and

A fall of Nothingness!

Back they must go then

From this dawn's edge or die,

When: through clouds

Their luminosities and

Colorations of mist,

A thrust of sun, and

There across, the Castle

Of the Great Khan!

An instant, then

A savage and watchful wind

Boiled from the Chasm,

And all was shifty blind

Insidious refraction,

Sensory error, echo bar --

A dawn of prisms for

An impossible day!

Still he maintained:

"Did you not see?" "I did !"

Then was it not absolute

As two to none?

There they must cross

By ledge of dawn or die

Tentatively till they fall --

But wait for noon.

ooooooooooooooooooooo

"Can you not logic for me
A bridge of hairs? I'll use it
To join that peril to these
That I daily use --

The dear lap-adder
Of my common sense,
My chamber-wolves
Philosophy and Science.

These shy, discursive beasts
Stand in my path.
'Why so demonstrative?'
And they, baring:

'Prince, you are
Malingering on a brink
Of meaningless night wherein
Thought swirls and is lost!'"

Then I your presumptuous finch

Circled out over the Chasm

Wickedly: "This is a cloud

Of some scope. Oh do you balk

At the first and very step?

It would be hair-raising

To the featherless, unless

One were a prince. . . .

If one could walk partially

Into space, palpate for purchase,

Test for solids, and

In a decent light!

No one will push a prince;

Nor will your own ground

Crumble suddenly beneath you ---"

"I'd like that, my needle!

For suppose I do not dare

Your flying leap: Then

Why was I not

More pleasantly unprepared?"

"Surely," She said, "the object was

Not to prepare us for

A habit that would prevail

During normal times,

But to act now, in

This emergency?" He:

"There are no normal times,

Only this fatal now!"

"Nothing so simple

As simplicity, or

So simple to find.

One does not achieve it,

One accepts it,

Or rather falls heir

To it, so to say, as

To a contested legacy."

"All that is required"

(Flirting, the sallow bird)

"Is the exhaustion of

Alternatives, pocket and pouch."

"This fluttering thing
Without rank consoles me
When I am alone --
It has no real weight. . . . .

What if I sauntered carelessly
Along this brink, turning
My back on strangers?
Nothing would happen.

But no one would
Call me back, either!
All is, as I would have it,
Disinterested.

My absence, like my
Presence here, offends.
This is a place of
Deep embarrassment. . . .

It may be, I can
Spin out webs or a chain
To my advantage, and

Bring it, as it were,

Closer, to improve
The precipice -- though
My bones be lighter than birds
And my flesh Air. . . .

This Lady does not speak,
Yet She says to me:
'Prince, if you must think
Think Love, and leap.'

Can there be no
Translation of the word
I must now reply
In the language of events?

A prince is supposed to be
All gift when the time comes.
Lady, goodbye. . . .
Yet, I have no heir!

On this unpromising brim ˙
Where discipline fails,

Conditions could not

Be more ideal."

°°°°°°°°°°°°°°°°°°°°°°°

A humoring lazulite

In a granite sky,

A waking eye in love:

Noon and a point of view --

Wherein we looked

Instantly but well:

Did we not see, we three,

Castle and Khan?

A gleam of arms:

Pensive but on watch

He stood his tour

As always rigormost

Nightly sentry in his own command

Shading his eyes

Now by noon the Great Khan

Watches for the truant Prince --

And for Kaliya
Thirsting on the Abyss. . . .
Grizzled winds from the Ditch
Bolt shut the black sky.

ooooooooooooooooooooooo

"Guilt is my staple
Undiminishing loaf
On which I batten
And grow thin.

My ribs do show
Subtle distinctions
As between
Life and death.

Abandoning all,
I am possessed.
I hear voices, hammering,
Buzzing and bells.

In every flowing branch

Of man or tree, I hear
The Minstrel singing
To himself in me.

I would unfold to
Himself these depths
These shifting surfaces,
To become

A single, simple
Listening device.
I would be all surface,
Like sand, which is

Implicit wholly in
Its exterior, which
Both contains and
Relinquishes all."

All of Night
Charged from the Abyss,
Claimed for the Rebel
The Provenance of Air

From the irresolute Prince.

The Sun recoiled,

Dealt a last white light

At infamy, and fell.

My flare of wound

Departingly but well, o

Eye to eye the Prince met

The gaze of the Great Khan!

°°°°°°°°°°°°°°°°°°°°°°°°

"I am a don of

Multitudinous sense,

And every sense has

A pit, and every pit

A branch of learning

And a chair of Death.

In this academy

I matriculate."

"A message comes

For you to volunteer

For acts requiring a degree

Of impartiality. . . ."

"I go," the Prince said,

"This pitch is so thick,

That what unnerved me

In the visible,

Space, is now

An unseen hypothesis.

The blind have a sense

Of distance. From this rock

It is not far."

So light and strong was he,

And so full of desire:

He ran, and leaped!

Permit me not
To recount familiarly
Of what unfolds,
Since it is not a vision

Compassed but a
Unity apprehended.
I have taken no vows.
My theme is princely love.

ABOUT THE AUTHOR

John Berry was born and educated in Southern California. He taught at the University of Southern California, and for several years at Viswa Bharati University in India. *Krishna Fluting*, his first novel, won the 1959 Macmillan Fiction Award and was a Book-of-the-Month Club selection. Macmillan also published a story collection, *Flight of White Crows*, 1961; Gollanz in England, 1962. His work appeared in many fiction and poetry journals; stories in *New World Writing*, *The Noble Savage*, *Harper's Magazine*, *Prairie Schooner*, *Massachusetts Review*, *Chelsea*, *Denver Quarterly*, and others. He was awarded the Phelan Fellowship for Poetry, two MacDowell Fellowships, an Ingram Merrill grant for poetry, a Guggenheim and a Fullbright.

For several decades before his sudden death in 2000, he collaborated with his artist wife on sculpture. Many of the bronze sculptures he worked on have been exhibited in museums throughout the country including The Fresno Art Museum, California, The Kennedy Museum of American Art, Ohio, and the Lyman Allyn Art Museum, Connecticut. He continued to write during most of this period. He finished the final version of *Travels of the Prince* in 1997.

5850

Printed in the United States
704600003B